MW00915111

Small Catechism of the Orthodox Church

of

1649

Translated by

Anonymous

First English Edition 2024

Small Catechism

Originally published in 1649 in Moscow

Translated by Anonymous

This work is in the public domain.

No rights reserved.

This edition typeset in LaTeX by Old Believer Books

2024

Cover image: St. John the Theologian. 15th Century.

Contents

A Collection of Brief Teachings on the Articles of Faith.

That is, concerning the dogmas or traditions of faith of the Orthodox, Catholic, and Christian Church. For an article, in Slavic, is interpreted as a tradition or a composition: in accordance with the confession and teaching of the Holy Eastern Apostolic Catholic Church, for the instruction and knowledge of all Orthodox Christians, especially for children learning, by the command of His Majesty Tsar and Grand Prince Alexei Mikhailovich, Sovereign of all Rus', and by the blessing of His Eminence, the Most Holy Patriarch Joseph of Moscow and all Rus'. It was published in print in the Slavic language in the reigning city of Moscow, in the year 7157 (1649 AD), on the 20th day of January.

This was printed in full agreement with the aforementioned book of the Catechism, with the first printing from the Christian printing house at the Preobrazhensky almshouse in Moscow, in the year 7418 (1910 AD).

The Symbol, or Confession, of the Most Blessed Afanasiy, Patriarch of Alexandria.

Whoever desires to be saved must, above all, hold the Catholic faith. Anyone who does not keep it whole and undefiled will, without doubt, perish eternally. This is the Catholic faith: that we venerate one God in Trinity, and Trinity in Unity, neither confusing the Persons nor dividing the Essence. For there is one Person of the Father, another of the Son, and another of the Holy Ghost. But the Godhead of the Father, the Son, and the Holy Ghost is one, their glory equal, their majesty coeternal. As the Father is, so is the Son, and so is the Holy Ghost: the Father uncreated, the Son uncreated, and the Holy Ghost uncreated; the Father incomprehensible, the Son incomprehensible, and the Holy Ghost incomprehensible. The Father eternal, the Son eternal, and the Holy Ghost eternal. And yet there are not three eternals but one eternal. Likewise, there are not three incomprehensibles or three uncreated, but one uncreated and one incomprehensible. Similarly, the Father is almighty, the Son almighty, and the Holy Ghost almighty; and yet they are not three almighties but one almighty. So the Father is God, the Son is God, and the Holy Ghost is God; yet they are not three Gods but one God. Likewise, the Father is Lord, the Son is Lord, and the Holy Ghost is Lord; and yet they are not three Lords but one Lord. For as we are compelled by Christian truth to acknowledge each Person individually as both God and Lord, so we are forbidden by the Catholic religion to say that there are three Gods or three Lords. The Father is made of none, neither created nor begotten. The Son is from the Father alone, not made nor created, but begotten. The Holy Ghost is neither made, nor created, nor begotten, but proceeds. So there is one Father, not three Fathers; one Son, not three Sons; one Holy Ghost, not three Holy Ghosts. And in this Trinity, none is before or after, none is greater or less, but the whole three Persons are coeternal and coequal. In every way, as was said before, the Trinity in Unity and Unity in Trinity is to be worshiped. Therefore, whoever desires to be saved must think thus of the Trinity.

Concerning Christ.

It is necessary, however, for eternal salvation that one also believe faithfully in the Incarnation of our Lord Jesus Christ. The true faith is that we believe and confess that our Lord Jesus Christ, the Son of God, is both God and man. He is God, begotten from the substance of the Father before all ages, and He is man, born from the substance of His mother in time. Perfect God and perfect man, composed of a rational soul and human flesh, equal to the Father in His divinity, less than the Father in His humanity. Although He is God and man, He is not two, but one Christ. One, not by turning the divinity into flesh, but by taking humanity into God; one altogether, not by confusion of substance, but by unity of person. For as the rational soul and flesh is one man, so God and man is one Christ. He suffered for our salvation, descended into hell, rose again on the third day from the dead, ascended into heaven, and sits at the right hand of God the Father Almighty. From there He will come to judge the living and the dead. At His coming, all men will rise with their bodies and will give an account of their deeds. Those who have done good will go into eternal life, and those who have done evil into everlasting fire.

This is the Catholic faith, which unless a man believes faithfully and firmly, he cannot be saved.

The Brief Exposition of Faith by the Blessed Patriarchs Anastasi of Great Antioch and Kyrill of Alexandria.

Questions and answers on theology.

Question: Of what faith are you?

Answer: I am a Christian.

Question: What is a Christian?

Answer: One who lives in God, and remains in piety and goodness.

Question: How many natures do you confess in theology?

Answer: I confess one nature.

Question: Which nature?

Answer: The Divine nature.

Question: What is God?

Answer: God is an independent being, the cause of all things; that is, He is all-powerful and omnipotent, transcending all causes and natures.

Question: How is the Father distinguished from the Son?

Answer: By their persons, for the Father is unbegotten.

Question: How is the Son distinguished from the Father?

Answer: By their persons, for the Son is begotten.

Question: How is the Holy Ghost distinguished from the Father and the Son?

Answer: By their persons, for the Holy Ghost proceeds.

Question: How do you believe?

Answer: I believe in one God, the Father, and in one Son, begotten of Him, and in one Holy Ghost, proceeding from the Father, who is God.

Question: What is a substance?

Answer: A substance is an independent thing, requiring nothing else for its formation.

Question: How many persons do you confess in the Divine nature?

Answer: I confess three persons: the Father, the Son, and the Holy Ghost.

Question: What is a person?

Answer: It forms the power of the single essence of the Father. However, when we speak of the persons of God, we refer to them as incorporeal and without form.

Question: What is distinct in each of the three persons, and what is common?

Answer: The Father's distinction is His unbegottenness; the Son's distinction is His begottenness; and the Holy Ghost's distinction is His procession. What they share in common is divinity and kingship.

Concerning Christ

Question: Regarding the incarnation of Christ, how many natures do you confess?

Answer: I confess two natures: one divine and one human.

Question: What is the divine will?

Answer: The divine will is to cleanse the leprous, as Christ demonstrated His divine will and action when He said to the leper: *I will, be thou clean.*[1]

Question: What is God's action?

Answer: God's action is the salvation of all people and the leading of them to the knowledge of the truth.

Question: What is the human will?

Answer: The human will is to request something, such as asking to drink, as Christ did on the cross.

Question: What is human action?

Answer: Human action includes walking along a path, becoming weary, and other such things.

Question: How many persons do you confess in the incarnation?

Answer: I confess one person, for He is both the Son of God and the Son of the Virgin.

Question: How is the Son a partaker with the Father and the Holy Ghost?

Answer: He partakes with them in His divine nature, for He is

---

[1]Matthew 8:3; Mark 1:41; Luke 5:13

perfect God.

Question: How is the Son a partaker with mankind?

Answer: In His human nature, for He is also perfect man.

Question: Why did the Son become incarnate, and not the Father or the Ghost?

Answer: So that the property of His hypostasis would be preserved, for He is to be both the Son in heaven and the Son on earth. Amen.

The Exposition of the Blessed St. Maxim on the Faith, briefly questioned and answered for every Orthodox Christian

Question: How many natures do you confess in the Most Holy, consubstantial, and indivisible Trinity?

Answer: I confess one nature.

Question: How many essences?

Answer: One essence.

Question: How many images?

Answer: One image.

Question: How many wills, or desires?

Answer: One will.

Question: How many persons, or faces?

Answer: I confess three persons: the Father, the Son, and the Holy Ghost.

Question: Who among the Holy Trinity was incarnated?

Answer: The Son, the Word.

Question: How many natures do you confess in the incarnate Son of God for our sake?

Answer: I confess two natures: divinity and humanity.

Question: How many essences?

Answer: I confess two essences: one consubstantial with the Father in divinity, and the other consubstantial with the mother in humanity.

Question: How many wills, or desires?

Answer: I confess two wills: the will of divinity and the will of humanity.

Question: How many actions?

Answer: I confess two actions.

Question: How many persons?

Answer: One person, God the Word.

Question: How many births?

Answer: I confess two births: the first is eternal, timeless, and bodiless, for He shone forth from the Father like light from the sun; the second birth occurred later, from the Holy Virgin God-bearer (Theotokos/Богородица) Mary, as the Great God, eternal, co-beginningless, invisible, incomprehensible, indescribable in His divinity, unchangeable, and who knows the hearts of all people. The Holy God-bearer bore one person, recognized in two natures. In His divinity, He was begotten eternally by the Father, and later, in time, was incarnated from her, born in the flesh. If those who inquire ask us whether He who was born from the Holy God-bearer is in two natures, we will say to them, *Yes, He is in two natures: He is both God and man.* Similarly, concerning the crucifixion, resurrection, and ascension, the natures shine forth, not the persons. Christ suffered in two natures, crucified in His human nature. For it was His flesh that hung on the cross, not His divinity. And if again they ask us, *Did two natures die?* We will say to them, *No, God forbid. For two natures were not crucified, but Christ, who is God the Word, became incarnate and was born. It was His flesh that was crucified, His flesh that suffered, and His flesh that died, while His divinity remained impassible.*

Question: How many natures hung on the cross?

Answer: Jesus, being in two natures, hung on the cross in His human nature, in the flesh, not in divinity. This exposition is known, and the true Israelite, in whom there is no guile, understands it. And if you still wish to know what God is and how to worship Him, listen, pay attention, and truly understand: the Father, the Son, and the Holy Ghost are one in holiness, one in will, one in wisdom, and one in power. Neither did one come before time, and the other afterward, but together the Father, the Son, and the Holy Ghost exist. The Son is in the Father, and the Spirit is in the Son. Their nature is united, and their divinity is one. They are distinguished by persons as three, yet they are one in unity, according to the essential Word. Therefore, when we speak of the Father, we glorify the Son, and when we confess the Holy Ghost, we call them God. God is the common divine essence of the Father, the Son, and the Holy Ghost. And when we say "Father, Son, and Holy Ghost," these are not common names, but personal to each person. For the Father is not called the Son, the Son is not called the Father, and the Holy Ghost is called neither Father nor Son. We confess three persons, or three faces, one image. We do not say that there are three substances or three natures or three gods, as the cursed disciples of Arius say, but one God. We confess one essence, one nature, in three persons. Nor do we say that there is one person, as the accursed Sabellians, but we confess three persons and three faces in one image, and in one divinity we confess, pray, and venerate.

The Book of Catechesis

That is, the Teaching on Faith and the Most Necessary Matters Pertaining to It

Question: Are there many things necessary for the salvation of an Orthodox Catholic Christian?

Answer: There are two things:[1] First, to have true faith in the Lord God, the one God in the Holy Trinity, and in everything that Christ taught in the Gospel. Second, to live piously according to the faith, as Holy Scripture teaches: *Ye see then how that of deeds a man is justified, and not of faith only.*[2] And elsewhere: *For as the body, without the spirit is deed, even so faith without works is dead also.* And in another place[3]: *having faith and good conscience: which some have put away from them, and as concerning faith have made shipwreck.* And in another place: *but holding the mystery of the faith with a pure conscience.*[4]

Question: Teach me why I must first have true faith, and then live piously according to that faith.

Answer: Because, as it is written, without faith it is impossible to please God, as the Holy Apostle Paul says: *He that cometh to God must believe that he is, and that he is a rewarder of them that diligently seek him.*[5]

Question: Where should I learn about faith and Christian pious living?

Answer: From Holy Scripture, the Apostolic Tradition, and also from the Holy Catholic Church, which in the councils

---

[1] Chrysostom, Homily 3
[2] James 2
[3] Chrysostom, Homily 3, 1 Timothy 1
[4] Chrysostom, Homily 3, 1 Timothy 1
[5] Hebrews 11:6

through the Holy Fathers has handed down perfect and true dogmas. But since it is difficult for everyone who desires to learn the Christian faith to immediately grasp it in full, a brief collection or exposition is offered here for ease of understanding.

Question: How many parts are there in this collection of teachings?

Answer: Three: The first is an exposition of the faith; the second, about hope; and the third, about love—love for God and for one's neighbor.

On Faith

Question: What is faith?

Answer: Faith, as the divine Apostle Paul says, is *the substance of things hoped for, the evidence of things not seen.*[1] Or, as Chrysostom says,

> faith is a firm and steadfast understanding, with boldness in the heart concerning God and matters of salvation, which we see with the heart though unseen, and confess with our mouths, as it is written: *For with the heart man believeth unto righteousness; and with the mouth confession is made unto salvation*[2].[3]

Question: How many compositions of faith are there?

Answer: According to the confession of the Christian faith composed at the two Ecumenical Councils—the First Nicene Council and the Second Council of Constantinople—there are twelve articles of the Orthodox Christian faith[4].

Question: What is the first article of the composition of faith?

---

[1] Hebrews 11:1

[2] Romans 10:10

[3] Chrysostom, Homily on Hebrews 11, Homily 32

[4] Council of Nicaea and Constantinople; Athanasius, Commentary on the Faith

Answer: *I believe in one God, the Father Almighty, Creator of heaven and earth, and all things visible and invisible.*

Question: How many things are contained in this article, and what do we learn from it?

Answer: Three things: First, we must believe and confess that God is one in His essence, but exists in three Persons, as follows: Father, Son, and Holy Ghost. These three Persons are one God, as Christ teaches in the Gospel, *Go ye therefore, and teach all nations, baptizing them in the name of the Father, and of the Son, and of the Holy Ghost.*[1] Second, this teaches that among the three divine Persons, the first Person, without beginning and without end, the source and root, and the cause of both, is the Father, begetting the Son, and from whom the Holy Ghost proceeds.[2]

Question: What is the second thing this article teaches?

Answer: It teaches that God is always one, without beginning or end, and that out of His goodness He is the creator of all things, both visible and invisible,[3] as Holy Scripture teaches: *Lord, Thou art God, which hast made heaven, and earth, and the sea, and all that in them is.*[4] And elsewhere: *For by Him were all things created, that are in heaven, and that are in earth, visible and invisible, whether thrones, or dominions, or principalities, or powers: all things were created by Him, and for Him.*[5]

Question: What is the third thing this article teaches?

Answer: It teaches that all created things, even the lowest

---

[1] Matthew 28:19
[2] Athanasius, Discourse Against the Arians; also in his Confession of Faith
[3] Damascene, Book 2, Chapter 2
[4] Acts 4:24
[5] Colossians 1:16

24

of them, are governed and preserved by God's power,[1] as it is written, *The eyes of all wait upon Thee; and Thou givest them their meat in due season. Thou openest Thine hand, and satisfiest the desire of every living thing.*[2]

Question: What else should I learn about God from this article?

Answer: You should understand that in God there are two properties: one is His essence, which is common to all three Persons, as to God the Father, the Son, and the Holy Ghost, when we speak of one God in Trinity. The second property is personal and not common, but particular to each Person: for instance, the Father begets the Son, and sends forth the Holy Ghost; the Son is begotten of the Father before all ages from His essence, and likewise the Holy Ghost proceeds from the same Father.

Question: What is the difference between personal properties and essence?

Answer: The property of essence signifies that there is one God, one essence, and one substance, as well as one glory, one throne, and one majesty.[3] The personal property, however, signifies the distinction of the three Persons in the one divinity without confusion: that the property of one Person cannot be transferred to another.

Question: How should I understand creation?

Answer: Every creation from God, in its essence, is made complete and very good, as it is written: *And God saw every thing that He had made, and, behold, it was very good.*[4]

---

[1] Damascene, Book 2, Chapter 2
[2] Psalm 144
[3] Damascene, Book 1, Chapter 9
[4] Genesis 1:31

Question: What did the Lord God create first?

Answer: As written by Moses, in the creation of this visible world, God first made heaven and earth; and at the end of all other creation, He made man from the dust of the ground, breathing into him the breath of life, and created him in His own image and likeness.[1]

Question: Did the Lord God create anything before this visible world?

Answer: The Holy Fathers, of the Eastern Churches, teach that before this visible world, invisible angels were created.[2] Man, however was created with two essences: one visible, having a body, and one invisible, having a soul.

Question: How should I understand angels?

Answer: Angels are intelligent spirits, free-willed beings, heavenly servants of the Lord Almighty,[3] as it is written, *Who maketh His angels spirits; His ministers a flaming fire.*[4]

Question: How many orders are the angels divided into?

Answer: There are nine orders of angels: thrones, cherubim, seraphim, principalities, powers, virtues, dominions, archangels, and angels.

Question: What is the service of the angels before God?

Answer: First, they continually glorify and serve the Lord

---

[1] Genesis 1:1

[2] Chrysostom, On Providence, Deserving of Honor, Book 1; Damascene, Book 2, Chapter 12; Gregory the Theologian, Discourse on the Unbegotten

[3] Damascene, Book 2, Chapter 3

[4] Psalm 103

God according to His holy will and command.[1] They are also intercessors for God's chosen people unto salvation, as it is written, *Are they not all ministering spirits, sent forth to minister for them who shall be heirs of salvation?*[2] They also announce God's will and His blessings to men, as the angel announced to the Most Holy Virgin, and as they proclaimed the birth of Christ to the shepherds at midnight.[3]

Question: How should I understand the angelic service to us?

Answer: They protect us from the enemy of our souls and from all evil, as Holy Scripture teaches, *But the angel of the Lord by night opened the prison doors, and brought them forth, and said, Go, stand and speak in the temple to the people all the words of this life.*[4] And elsewhere, *And when Peter was come to himself, he said, Now I know of a surety, that the Lord hath sent His angel, and hath delivered me out of the hand of Herod, and from all the expectation of the people of the Jews.*[5] Our prayers, alms, and other pious deeds are brought before the throne of God, as Holy Scripture testifies, *When thou didst pray with tears, and didst bury the dead, and didst leave thy dinner, and didst hide the dead by day in thine house, and bury them by night, I did bring thy prayer before the Lord.*[6]

Question: Does every person have a guardian angel?

Answer: Every believer has one, according to what is said in the Gospel: *Take heed that ye despise not one of these little ones; for I say unto you, That in heaven their angels do always behold the face*

---

[1] Dionysius, On the Celestial Hierarchy, Chapter 7
[2] Hebrews 1:14
[3] Luke 1, 2
[4] Acts 5:19-20
[5] Acts 12:11
[6] Tobit 12:12

of My Father which is in heaven. And not only people have them, but also cities, nations, and kingdoms, as well as monasteries and churches, each having their own special guardian angels.[1]

Question: How or by what means do we receive guardian angels?

Answer: Through continual prayer, asking them for intercession before the Lord God, especially one's own guardian angel, that he may bring our prayers before the throne of God and intercede for us, and be our helper against every enemy, especially the invisible one.

Question: How do we drive away our guardian angel?

Answer: By sins, especially mortal sins: if someone falls into sin, especially mortal sin, due to human weakness, he should not delay, but must quickly cleanse himself through confession and repentance, so that the guardian angel may return to us and not allow the invisible enemy to lead us into greater sins.[2]

Question: Are all angels holy and good?

Answer: All angels were created holy and good by the Lord God, but the rebel angel and those who shared his mindset voluntarily turned away from God and made themselves evil and deceitful, as Christ says: *He was a murderer from the beginning, and abode not in the truth, because there is no truth in him. When he speaketh a lie, he speaketh of his own: for he is a liar, and the father of it.*[3] For this, he was cast out of heaven, and instead of being an angel, he became Satan and the deceiver of mankind.

---

[1] Matthew 18:10; Damascene, Book 2, Chapter 3; Dionysius, On the Celestial Hierarchy, Chapter 9; Theophylact, Commentary on Matthew 18; Chrysostom, Homily on Disobedience

[2] Chrysostom, Homily on Matthew 4:5

[3] John 8:44

Question: Can the devil force a person to sin?

Answer: The devil, being the first enemy of man, always tempts him and leads him to sin by various means, as it is written: *Be sober, be vigilant; because your adversary the devil, as a roaring lion, walketh about, seeking whom he may devour.* However, he cannot compel us.[1]

Question: How should I understand man?

Answer: Man was created by the Lord God, in His image and likeness, as we have learned earlier. Before sin, man was in a state of innocence, not knowing what was evil, but when he transgressed God's commandment, he lost the state of sinlessness and became subject to weakness.[2]

Question: What is the difference between the state of sinlessness and the state of sin?

Answer: The state of sinlessness includes in itself, by grace, immortality and incorruptibility. The state of sin brought with it death and corruption, as it is written: *In the day that thou eatest thereof, thou shalt surely die.*[3]

Question: In what state was man after sin?

Answer: In death, corruption, and all passions, and under a curse, yet not without hope, for when the Lord God spoke to the serpent: *And I will put enmity between thee and the woman, and between thy seed and her seed; it shall bruise thy head, and thou shalt bruise his heel.*[4] This hope and God's promise comforted mankind, especially the patriarchs and prophets, until the

---

[1] 1 Peter 5:8; Damascene, Book 2, Chapter 4
[2] Basil the Great
[3] Damascene, Book 2, Chapter 1
[4] Genesis 3:15

coming of the Messiah. When the long-awaited Messiah, Jesus Christ, came according to the promise, He redeemed the human race with His blood from the power of the enemy, removed the curse, and granted immortality in eternal life, as we will learn further.

Question: Did God know that Adam would sin?

Answer: Not only about Adam, but also about the devil and all creation, He knew and was aware. I speak here of angels and humans, who think, speak, and act. However, all was created for the manifestation of His greater grace. In man, God also foresaw not only that His greater grace would be revealed through redemption, but also that it would be manifest in the very nature and person of the Son of God, who would sit at the right hand of the throne of God,[1] and the angels would worship Him as their Lord, and neither the malice of the devil nor human sin would be able to rule or harm the world again.[2]

Question: Does God oversee all of creation?

Answer: As it was said earlier, God knows all things. However, it must also be stated more clearly: the Lord God knows all, for He holds even the smallest things in His hand and governs them, as He Himself teaches in the Gospel: *Are not two sparrows sold for a farthing? And one of them shall not fall on the ground without your Father. But the very hairs of your head are all numbered.*[3]

Question: If the Lord God watches over man, why did He allow him to fall into sin?

Answer: The time in Paradise was appointed as a trial for man,

---

[1] Hebrews 1:3
[2] Damascene, Book 2, Chapter 4
[3] Matthew 10:29-30; Chrysostom, On Providence, Book 1

which was given by a commandment. Since he did not keep the commandment, not yet being established by grace, but left in his own free will, as it is written,

> He created man in the beginning and left him in the hand of his counsel; if thou wilt, to keep the commandments, and to perform acceptable faithfulness. He hath set fire and water before thee: stretch forth thy hand unto whether thou wilt. Before man is life and death; and whether him liketh shall be given him.[1]

Failing to give proper obedience and faith, man fell into sin by God's permission, as a means of demonstrating greater grace.

Question: What is God's providence for man in the state of sin?

Answer: The merciful God never abandons His providence over man, but always provides him with a way toward goodness. He does this without removing man's free will, but by assisting him with His grace. And by grace, I refer to the grace now given through Jesus Christ.[2]

Question: What else should I learn from this article?

Answer: Whatever better and more excellent thing your mind can comprehend, attribute all of it to the Lord God, who is the giver of every good thing. Regarding creation, understand that if a thing possesses goodness, it is from the Lord God. But if there is anything evil, it is from oneself, that is, from man and the wicked angels.[3]

---

[1] Sirach 15:14-17
[2] Damascene, Book 3, Chapter 3; Book 2, Chapters 9 and 27
[3] Damascene, Book 1, Chapter 12; James 1:17; Dionysius, On the Divine

Question: What is the second article of faith?

Answer: And in one Lord Jesus Christ, the only-begotten Son of God, begotten of the Father before all ages. Light from Light, true God from true God, begotten, but not created, of one essence with the Father, who wrought all things.

Question: What does this article teach us?

Answer: Two things: first, that the eternal Word, Jesus Christ, was begotten of God the Father and not created, and has existed with the Father before all ages, being of one essence and substance, sharing the same glory, throne, and majesty. He is true God of true God, uncreated Light from uncreated Light.[1]

Question: What else does this article teach?

Answer: It teaches that the entire visible and invisible world was created by this eternal Word, as Holy Scripture teaches, *He was in the world, and the world was made by Him, and the world knew Him not.*[2] And elsewhere: *Whom He hath appointed heir of all things, by whom also He made the worlds.*[3]

Question: What do the names "Jesus Christ" signify?

Answer: The name "Jesus" (Исус) was commonly used among the Jews before, but when the eternal Word, the only-begotten Son of God, took upon Himself human nature, this name was brought from heaven by the angel Gabriel, signifying the Savior[4], as the Evangelist Matthew writes: *And she shall bring forth a son, and thou shalt call His name Jesus: for He shall save His*

Names, Chapter 1

[1] Athanasius, Creed; Damascene, Book 1, Chapters 6 and 9
[2] John 1:10
[3] Hebrews 1:2
[4] Athanasius, Discourse 3, Against the Arians

people from their sins.[1] From that time, this name has become unique and chosen, in which human salvation is revealed, as it is written: *Neither is there salvation in any other: for there is none other name under heaven given among men, whereby we must be saved.*[2] This name is so honored that both angels, men, and even demons must revere it, as written by the Apostle Paul: *Wherefore God also hath highly exalted Him, and given Him a name which is above every name: that at the name of Jesus every knee should bow, of things in heaven, and things in earth, and things under the earth.*[3]

Question: In what way should we honor the name of Jesus?

Answer: First, by remembering it with all reverence and fear, piously recalling the sinless suffering of Christ. With sighs and prayers, we should ask that for the sake of His voluntary suffering, He forgives our sins and shows us mercy, both now and at the hour of our death, and on the day of His righteous judgment.[4]

Question: What does "Christ" mean?

Answer: "Christ" means "the Anointed One": just as in the Old Law, three ranks were anointed with oil—priests, kings, and prophets—so too Christ Jesus is the Anointed One of God.[5] He was not anointed with oil in His humanity, but by the Holy Ghost. God the Father anointed Him for these three offices, according to the prophecy of Isaiah and as spoken in the Gospel: *The Spirit of the Lord is upon Me, because He hath anointed Me to preach the gospel to the poor; He hath sent Me to heal the*

---

[1] Matthew 1:21
[2] Acts 4:12
[3] Philippians 2:9-10
[4] Damascene, Book 1
[5] Damascene, Homily on the Nativity of the God-bearer

brokenhearted, to preach deliverance to the captives, and recovering of sight to the blind, to set at liberty them that are bruised.[1] In this testimony, all three offices of Christ are depicted, and in Him they were fulfilled, as He Himself says afterward: *This day is this scripture fulfilled in your ears.*[2]

Question: Teach me about these three offices of Christ.

Answer: Christ is, first of all, a priest according to the order of Melchizedek, as the Apostle says about Him: *He was called of God an high priest after the order of Melchizedek.*[3] He is called a priest because He offered Himself as a sacrifice,[4] first symbolically through bread and wine for our purification, and later when He poured out His own blood, as the Apostle also says: *For if the blood of bulls and of goats, and the ashes of an heifer sprinkling the unclean, sanctifieth to the purifying of the flesh: how much more shall the blood of Christ, who through the eternal Spirit offered Himself without spot to God, purge your conscience from dead works to serve the living God?*[5] He is also called the eternal King, as the angel declared: *And the Lord God shall give unto Him the throne of His father David: and He shall reign over the house of Jacob for ever; and of His kingdom there shall be no end.*[6] The title placed on His cross also bears witness to this: *Jesus of Nazareth, the King of the Jews.*[7] Finally, His prophetic office is signified by everything He preached and taught, which reveals the prophetic nature of His mission.

Question: Why is He called the Only-Begotten Son of God?

---

[1] Isaiah 61:1; Luke 4:18
[2] Luke:21
[3] Hebrews 5:10
[4] Chrysostom, Homily 8, On the Priesthood, Book 5
[5] Hebrews 9:13-14
[6] Luke 1:32-33
[7] John 19:19

Answer: For two reasons:[1] first, because of the distinction between the Son's hypostasis and that of the Holy Ghost, who proceeds from God the Father, but not by way of begetting, rather by procession. He is called the Only-Begotten in distinction from the sons who are named only by grace, such as the faithful and the elect of God. By nature, Jesus Christ alone is called the Only-Begotten Son of God, for He was begotten from the substance and person of the Father before all ages, without beginning.[2]

Question: What is the third article of faith?

Answer: *For us men, and for our salvation, came he down from heaven and was incarnate of the Holy Ghost, and of the Virgin Mary became man.*

Question: What does this article teach?

Answer: Four things: first, that the eternal Son of God, for the sake of human salvation, by the goodwill of God the Father and the Holy Ghost, came down to earth.[3] He did not descend from one place to another, for as God He is everywhere and fills all things, but He humbled Himself and became man, as the holy Apostle Paul says: *Who, being in the form of God, thought it not robbery to be equal with God: But made Himself of no reputation, and took upon Him the form of a servant, and was made in the likeness of men.*[4] He did not transform His divinity into humanity, nor did He transform humanity into divinity, but being true God, He took on perfect humanity, and thus became both God and man in one person, keeping the properties

---

[1]Chrysostom, On the Incomprehensible, Homily 1; John 1:18

[2]Damascene, Book 4, Chapter 8

[3]Damascene, Book 3, Chapters 1 and 2; Athanasius, Homily on the Incarnation

[4]Philippians 2:6-7

of both natures intact.[1] Thus, He is true God and true man, as the Apostle Paul clearly teaches: *Great is the mystery of godliness: God was manifest in the flesh.*[2]

Question: What is the second thing this article teaches?

Answer: It teaches that Christ did not bring human nature with Him from heaven, but through the action of the Holy Ghost, He took it from the most pure Virgin Mary at the time of the Annunciation by the archangel, where she replied, saying: *Behold the handmaid of the Lord; be it unto me according to thy word.*[3] And with the word of the archangel, the perfect divinity of the Son of God, united with perfect humanity, was conceived in the womb of the most pure Virgin: as He was begotten of God the Father before all ages according to His divinity, so He was born of His mother in time, perfect in body and soul according to His humanity.[4]

Question: What is the third thing this article teaches?

Answer: That the conception of the Son of God in the womb of the Virgin, according to His humanity, was accomplished by the action of the Holy Ghost, as the angel explains when he says to the Virgin: *The Holy Ghost shall come upon thee, and the power of the Highest shall overshadow thee: therefore also that holy thing which shall be born of thee shall be called the Son of God.*[5] And elsewhere it is written: *The angel of the Lord appeared unto him in a dream, saying, Joseph, thou son of David, fear not to take unto thee Mary thy wife: for that which is conceived in her is of the*

---

[1] Basil the Great, On the Nature of Christ, Chapter 5; Damascene, Book 3, Chapter 3

[2] 1 Timothy 3:16

[3] Luke 1:38

[4] Damascene, Book 3, Chapter 2

[5] Luke 1:35

Holy Ghost.[1] Therefore, the most pure Virgin Mary was a virgin both before conception, in conception, and after conception; and thus she remained a virgin before, during, and after the birth, and became the most pure God-bearer.[2]

Question: What is the fourth thing this article teaches?

Answer: It teaches about the most pure Virgin, that she, chosen before all ages and prefigured from generations past, being the mother of the Son of God, should be venerated and glorified by us with divine honor.

Question: How should I venerate, magnify, and glorify the most pure Virgin?

Answer: Although there are many forms of honoring God's chosen saints, we should understand the veneration of the most pure Virgin as the Holy Eastern Catholic and Apostolic Church teaches. The Virgin God-bearer must be honored and exalted not only above all the saints but also above all the angelic ranks, above the cherubim and seraphim.[3] After God Himself, she is to be regarded with the highest honor, as is testified by her own words in the Holy Gospel: *For, behold, from henceforth all generations shall call me blessed.*[4] Therefore, every day we are obliged, not only in our prayers but also outside of them, to repeat the angelic greeting or Annunciation, saying: *Virgin Mother of God, rejoice Mary, full of grace, the Lord is with thee; blessed art thou among women, and blessed is the fruit of thy womb: for thou hast borne Christ the Savior, the Deliverer of our souls.*

---

[1] Matthew 1:20

[2] Damascene, Book 3, Chapter 3

[3] Damascene, Homilies on the Nativity and Dormition of the God-bearer

[4] Luke 1:48

Question: How should I understand this greeting?

Answer: First, know that this greeting was not devised by human thought but was brought from heaven by the archangel Gabriel from the Lord God.[1] For the angel would never have dared to announce such tidings to the Virgin unless he had been commanded by God. The second part of the greeting comes from the holy Elizabeth, who, being filled with the Holy Ghost and prophesying, spoke to this same Virgin and God-bearer, as the Evangelist Luke testifies. The Church also added certain words to this greeting from her own authority.[2]

Question: What is the teaching contained in this greeting?

Answer: First, in this greeting, we remember the Incarnation of God the Word. Whenever this greeting is spoken, it condemns all heretics who do not confess the true incarnation of the Lord Christ from the most pure Virgin. Likewise, it condemns the Nestorians, who do not call the most pure Virgin the God-bearer (Theotokos/Богородица). In this greeting, by remembering and honoring the most pure God-bearer, we frequently acquire her intercession before her Son and our God, that He may deliver us from our sins, as well as from visible and invisible enemies. Therefore, we ought to say this greeting often, especially during akafists and prayer services, so that she, covering us with her omophor, may protect us from all evil.

Question: What is the fourth article?

Answer: *And was crucified also for us under Pontius Pilate, and suffered, and was buried.*

Question: What are the many things we learn from this article?

---

[1] Luke 1:28
[2] Third Council, of Ephesus

Answer: Six things: First, just as Christ truly took human nature from the most pure Virgin, so too did He truly suffer and die in that human nature, as the Gospel testifies concerning Him: *And when Jesus had cried with a loud voice, He said, Father, into Thy hands I commend My spirit: and having said thus, He gave up the ghost.*

Question: What is the second thing we learn from this article?

Answer: That Christ the Lord, being without sin, suffered and died as a lamb for the remission of our sins, and poured out His precious blood, as the holy Apostle Peter says: *Forasmuch as ye know that ye were not redeemed with corruptible things, as silver and gold, from your vain conversation received by tradition from your fathers; but with the precious blood of Christ, as of a lamb without blemish and without spot.*[1]

Question: What is the third thing this article teaches?

Answer: It teaches that Christ suffered only in His human nature on the cross, while His divinity suffered nothing,[2] as the Apostle Paul says: *In the body of His flesh through death, to present you holy and unblameable and unreproveable in His sight.*[3] If it may be said beautifully, *God suffered in the flesh.*

Question: What is the fourth thing this article teaches?

Answer: It teaches that Christ's suffering was greater than that of any man, as the prophet foretold in the person of Christ: *Is it nothing to you, all ye that pass by? Behold, and see if there be any sorrow like unto My sorrow.*[4] Christ's death was supreme because He offered Himself as a pure sacrifice for the people, as

---

[1] 1 Peter 1:18-19
[2] Damascene, Book 3, Chapter 8
[3] Colossians 1:22
[4] Lamentations 1:12

39

the Apostle Paul says: *And hath given Himself for us an offering and a sacrifice to God for a sweetsmelling savour.*[1] And elsewhere: *Who gave Himself a ransom for all.*[2]

Question: What is the fifth thing this article teaches?

Answer: It teaches that the Son of God truly died as a man and was buried by prominent and noble men of the Jewish nation, Joseph and Nicodemus.[3] Furthermore, His body was placed in a tomb, sealed, and guarded, which made His resurrection from the dead even more remarkable. His tomb was glorified according to prophecy, and to this day, anyone who comes to it with reverence and true faith can receive the remission of many sins.[4]

Question: What is the sixth thing this article teaches?

Answer: It teaches that in Christ's death, His divinity did not separate from either His soul or His body;[5] rather, His soul, with His divinity, descended into Hades and brought out all the holy fathers, leading them into Paradise along with the repentant thief. At the same time, by the unity of His divinity, He was enthroned with God the Father and the Holy Ghost in heaven, while His body was on the cross and in the tomb.

Question: Since you have mentioned the cross on which the Son of God suffered in the flesh, teach me how I should understand it.

Answer: Since we have mentioned the cross,[6] it should be held

---

[1] Ephesians 5:2
[2] 1 Timothy 2:6
[3] Matthew 27
[4] Damascene, Homily on the Sabbath
[5] Damascene, Book 3, Chapter 29
[6] Cyril of Jerusalem, Catechetical Lecture 13

in the highest honor and always remembered, for it was through the cross that Christ the Lord accomplished our salvation. As the Apostle Paul himself says when boasting about it: *But God forbid that I should glory, save in the cross of our Lord Jesus Christ, by whom the world is crucified unto me, and I unto the world.*[1] In this same way, every Christian should glory in the Holy Cross and frequently make use of its sign, bearing its mark on themselves, in church, at home, and while traveling.[2] In every action, let the sign of the Holy Cross be made first, especially when beginning prayers, eating, and drinking. Since the enemy of our souls cannot bear the sight of this cross, through which Christ was crucified for the salvation of man, he flees from us and cannot harm us.[3]

Question: How should I make the sign of the Holy Cross upon myself?

Answer: You should join the three fingers of your right hand together—the thumb, the little finger, and the finger next to the little one—confessing in them the mystery of the divine Trinity, the Father, the Son, and the Holy Ghost, one God in three persons. The two remaining fingers—the index and middle fingers—are stretched out to signify the mystery of our Lord Jesus Christ, who is both perfect God and perfect man for our salvation. After joining the fingers, place your hand first on your forehead, confessing that Christ is the one true and eternal Head, as the Apostle says: *God the Father has made Christ the head over all things to the church, which is His body.*[4] Then place your hand on your stomach, confessing His descent to earth and His conception without seed in the pure womb of the

---

[1] Galatians 6:14

[2] Damascene, Book 4, Chapter 12

[3] Chrysostom, Homily Against Eunomius and in many places

[4] Ephesians 1:22

God-bearer, for He passed through her womb as the sun passes through glass, without harming the seal of the Virgin in His birth. Then place your hand on your right shoulder, confessing that He sits at the right hand of God the Father, awaiting when His enemies are made His footstool. Finally, place your hand on your left shoulder, signifying that He will come again to judge the world, granting eternal life to those on His right and eternal punishment to those on His left. When crossing yourself with the sign of the cross, say this prayer: *Lord Jesus Christ, Son of God, have mercy on me, a sinner*, finishing with *Amen*, and bowing down to God, asking that He deliver us from the standing on the left and grant us His blessing.

Question: What is the fifth article of faith?

Answer: *And the third day He rose again after the Scriptures.*

Question: What does this article teach?

Answer: Two things: First, that just as the Son of God died of His own will, so by the power of His divinity, He also rose from the dead by His own will, according to His true word, where He says: *Therefore doth My Father love Me, because I lay down My life, that I might take it again. No man taketh it from Me, but I lay it down of Myself. I have power to lay it down, and I have power to take it again.*[1] This was in accordance with the writings of the holy prophets, as He Himself says: *Ought not Christ to have suffered these things, and to enter into His glory? And beginning at Moses and all the prophets, He expounded unto them in all the Scriptures the things concerning Himself.*[2]

Question: What is the second thing this article teaches?

---

[1] John 10:17-18
[2] Luke 24:26-27

Answer: It teaches that Christ rose from the dead in the same body in which He suffered and died.[1] The wounds in His hands, feet, and side bore witness to this, which He showed to His disciples after His resurrection, saying: *Behold My hands and My feet, that it is I Myself: handle Me, and see; for a spirit hath not flesh and bones, as ye see Me have.*[2] However, that body was glorified with glory and no longer subject to human weakness as it had been before death.

Question: What is the sixth article of faith?

Answer: *And ascended into heaven, and sitteth at the right hand of the Father.*

Question: What does this article teach?

Answer: Four things:[3] First, that the same body the Son of God received from the most pure Virgin, in which He suffered, died, and rose again, in that same body, He ascended into heaven with glory after His resurrection.[4] As the Evangelist Luke testifies: *And when He had spoken these things, while they beheld, He was taken up; and a cloud received Him out of their sight.*[5] He sits at the right hand of God the Father, as the Evangelist Mark also testifies: *So then after the Lord had spoken unto them, He was received up into heaven, and sat on the right hand of God.*[6]

Question: What is the second thing this article teaches?

Answer: It teaches that Christ ascended into heaven with His body, for as to His divinity, He was always with the Father and

---

[1] Damascene, Book 14, Chapter 58
[2] Luke 24:39
[3] Damascene, Homily on the Ascension of the Lord
[4] Damascene, Book 4, Chapter 1
[5] Acts 1:9
[6] Mark 16:19; Damascene, Book 4, Chapter 2

was never separated from Him, being of the same essence as the Father, as the Evangelist John testifies: *No man hath seen God at any time; the only begotten Son, which is in the bosom of the Father, He hath declared Him.*[1] By being in the bosom of the Father, it is understood that He is of the same essence with Him.

Question: What is the third thing this article teaches?

Answer: It teaches that He will never again part from the body which He once assumed, but will have it forever, as it is written: *Jesus Christ the same yesterday, and today, and forever.*[2]

Question: What is the fourth thing this article teaches?

Answer: It teaches that Christ is in heaven with His body and not everywhere according to the Apostle's word: *Christ sits at the right hand of God.*[3] Except, of course, for the most holy mysteries, where under the appearance of bread, it is His true body, and under the appearance of wine, His true blood, which comes to be through the descent of the Holy Ghost upon the gifts, invoked by the priest. There will be further teaching about this in its proper place.

Question: What is the seventh article of faith?

Answer: *And He shall come again with glory to judge the living and the dead, whose Kingdom has no end.*[4]

Question: What does this article teach?

Answer: Three things: first, that Christ will come again to earth to judge the living and the dead, not in humility and lowliness as before, but in glory and majesty, as He Himself says: *And*

---

[1] John 1:18
[2] Hebrews 13:8; Athanasius, On the Incarnation of the Word
[3] Colossians 3:1; Damascene, Book 4, Chapter 4
[4] Acts 1:11; Luke 1:33

they shall see the Son of Man coming in the clouds of heaven with power and great glory. Before His coming, well-known signs will precede it, as we hear in the Gospel of Matthew.

Question: What is the second thing this article teaches?

Answer: It teaches that on the last day of God's righteous judgment, people will give an account of all their thoughts, idle words, and deeds,[1] as the Savior Himself teaches: *But I say unto you, that every idle word that men shall speak, they shall give account thereof in the day of judgment.*[2]

Question: What is the third thing this article teaches?

Answer: It teaches that on the last day, everyone will receive according to their works. Some will inherit the kingdom of heaven, to whom it will be said: *Come, ye blessed of My Father, inherit the kingdom prepared for you from the foundation of the world.*[3] Others will go to eternal torment, to whom it will be said: *Depart from Me, ye cursed, into everlasting fire, prepared for the devil and his angels.*[4]

Question: What is the eighth article of faith?

Answer: *And in the Holy Ghost, the true and life-giving Lord, who proceedeth from the Father, who with the Father and the Son together is worshiped and glorified, who spake by the prophets.*

Question: What does this article teach?

Answer: Three things:[5] First, that the Holy Ghost is truly God,

---

[1] Damascene, Homily on the Dead
[2] Matthew 12:36
[3] Matthew 25:34
[4] Matthew 25:41
[5] Damascene, Book 1, Chapter 1; Basil the Great, Homily on the Holy Ghost

of the same essence as God the Father and the Son, sharing the same power, glory, and majesty. As the Apostle Paul teaches us, *There are diversities of gifts, but the same Spirit. And there are differences of administrations, but the same Lord. And there are diversities of operations, but it is the same God which worketh all in all.*[1]

Question: What is the second thing this article teaches?

Answer: It teaches that the Holy Ghost proceeds from the Father alone, as from the source and root in the Godhead, from His essence before all ages,[2] according to the teaching of the Savior: *But when the Comforter is come, whom I will send unto you from the Father, even the Spirit of truth, which proceedeth from the Father, He shall testify of Me.*[3] Thus, the Lord taught, the apostles preached, and the councils and holy fathers declared. For this faith, many martyrs suffered.

Question: What is the third thing this article teaches?

Answer: It teaches that in both the Old and New Testaments, the prophets and apostles declared that the Holy Ghost is the inspirer and giver of Holy Scripture: *For the prophecy came not in old time by the will of man: but holy men of God spake as they were moved by the Holy Ghost,*[4] according to the apostolic teaching.[5]

Question: How many gifts of the Holy Ghost are there?

Answer: Seven, as described by the prophet Isaiah and the holy

---

[1] 1 Corinthians 12:4-6; Athanasius, Creed; Dionysius, On the Divine Names

[2] Second Ecumenical Council; Dionysius, On the Divine Names, Chapter 2

[3] John 15:26; Damascene, Book 1, Chapters 8-10

[4] Athanasius, On the Incarnation of the Word

[5] 1 Peter 1:21

John in his Revelation.[1]

Question: What is the first gift of the Holy Ghost?

Answer: Wisdom, which is given from heaven in the knowledge of divine things, about which Scripture teaches us: *But the wisdom that is from above is first pure, then peaceable, gentle, and easy to be intreated, full of mercy and good fruits, without partiality, and without hypocrisy.*[2] This is contrary to the wisdom of this world, which is foolishness before God, as the Apostle Paul says, *Hath not God made foolish the wisdom of this world?*[3]

Question: What is the second gift of the Holy Ghost?

Answer: Understanding of the mysteries of faith and the will of God, as Scripture teaches us: *And the Lord gave wisdom and understanding in all manner of workmanship.*[4] And the Apostle says to Timothy: *The Lord give thee understanding in all things.*[5] Contrary to this is hardness of heart and lack of understanding toward faith and knowledge, as the Savior says: *O fools, and slow of heart to believe all that the prophets have spoken.*[6]

Question: What is the third gift of the Holy Ghost?

Answer: Counsel: when God gives someone the ability to advise both themselves and others in things that lead to salvation, as the Apostle teaches: *For I have not shunned to declare unto you all the counsel of God.*[7] The opposite of this is ungodly counsel, of which the prophet says: *Blessed is the man that walketh not in*

---

[1] Isaiah 11:2; Revelation 4:5; Theophylact, Commentary on Matthew 12
[2] James 3:17
[3] 1 Corinthians 1:20, 2:6
[4] Exodus 36:1
[5] 2 Timothy 2:7
[6] Luke 24:25
[7] Acts 20:27

the counsel of the ungodly.[1]

Question: What is the fourth gift of the Holy Ghost?

Answer: Fortitude, or courage in true faith and in a godly life, about which Scripture teaches us: *Watch ye, stand fast in the faith, quit you like men, be strong.*[2] The opposite of this is the fear of the ungodly, about which Scripture says: *There were they in great fear, where no fear was.*[3]

Question: What is the fifth gift of the Holy Ghost?

Answer: Knowledge of the law and will of God, about which the prophet speaks in the person of God: *I will give you pastors according to Mine heart, which shall feed you with knowledge and understanding.*[4] The opposite of this is ignorance and lack of knowledge of God and His law, about which it is written in the Psalms: *Pour out Thy wrath upon the heathen that have not known Thee, and upon the kingdoms that have not called upon Thy name.*[5]

Question: What is the sixth gift of the Holy Ghost?

Answer: Piety, which is always seen in a good and godly faith, in prayer, and in reflecting on the good works of God. The Apostle says about it: *For godliness is profitable unto all things, having promise of the life that now is, and of that which is to come.*[6] The opposite of this is all ungodliness, which has neither faith nor virtue.

---

[1] Psalm 1:1
[2] 1 Corinthians 16:13
[3] Psalm 52
[4] Jeremiah 3:15
[5] Psalm 78
[6] 1 Timothy 4:8

Question: What is the seventh gift of the Holy Ghost?

Answer: The fear of God, which is called filial fear, about which the Psalms say: *O fear the Lord, ye His saints.*[1] The opposite of this is either not fearing God at all or fearing Him as a servant, as the Apostle says: *There is no fear in love, but perfect love casteth out fear: because fear hath torment. He that feareth is not made perfect in love.*[2] Filial fear, a gift of the Holy Ghost, is to have a firm faith in the Lord God and to observe His holy commandments without stumbling.

Question: How many fruits of the Holy Ghost are there?

Answer: Every virtue and all godliness are called the fruits of the Holy Ghost, as it is written: *For the fruit of the Spirit is in all goodness and righteousness and truth.*[3] Elsewhere the Apostle enumerates the fruits of the Spirit, saying: *But the fruit of the Spirit is love, joy, peace, longsuffering, gentleness, goodness, faith, meekness, temperance: against such there is no law.*[4]

Question: What is the ninth article of faith?

Answer: *In one holy, catholic, and apostolic Church.*

Question: What does this article teach?

Answer: Four things: first, that the one holy catholic and apostolic Church is the bride of Christ, as the holy Apostle Paul says: *For I have espoused you to one husband, that I may present you as a chaste virgin to Christ.*[5] There is also one faith, one baptism, and one God. Furthermore, the Church is the one true

---

[1] Psalm 33
[2] 1 John 4:18
[3] Ephesians 5:9
[4] Galatians 5:22-23
[5] 2 Corinthians 11:2; Ephesians 4:4

and only Church.

Question: What is the Church?

Answer: The Church is the assembly of the faithful of God, united in the name of our Lord Jesus Christ, in the confession of faith, and in the apostolic teaching throughout the world, as members of one body of Christ, under one head, our Lord Jesus Christ, and in rightful obedience to Him. [1]

Question: What is the second thing this article teaches?

Answer: It teaches that this catholic Church does not receive its name from any man, but from Christ Himself, who redeemed her with His precious blood and betrothed her to Himself forever.[2] He alone is her head, as she is His eternal body.

Question: Which Church was the first?

Answer: The first Church was the Church of Jerusalem, for it is the mother and teacher of all other churches, as the Scripture testifies: *And that repentance and remission of sins should be preached in His name among all nations, beginning at Jerusalem.*[3] And elsewhere it is written: *When therefore Paul and Barnabas had no small dissension and disputation with them, they determined that Paul and Barnabas, and certain other of them, should go up to Jerusalem unto the apostles and elders about this question.*[4] And again: *And as they went through the cities, they delivered them the decrees for to keep, that were ordained of the apostles and elders which were at Jerusalem. And so were the churches established in the faith, and increased in number*

---

[1] Ephesians 5:23-24
[2] Chrysostom, Homily on Psalm 43
[3] Luke 24:47
[4] Acts 15:2

daily.[1]

Question: What is the third thing this article teaches?

Answer: It teaches that the foundation and head is no one else but Christ alone, as the holy Scripture teaches: *For other foundation can no man lay than that is laid, which is Jesus Christ.*[2] *And hath put all things under His feet, and gave Him to be the head over all things to the church, which is His body.*[3] And elsewhere: *For the husband is the head of the wife, even as Christ is the head of the church.*[4]

Question: What is the fourth thing this article teaches?

Answer: It teaches that we must give every obedience and submission to the holy Church as to our mother, according to the commandment of Christ, who said: *If he shall neglect to hear them, tell it unto the church: but if he neglect to hear the church, let him be unto thee as a heathen man and a publican.*[5] The Church has this honor from Christ, that she not only corrects laypeople but also clergy, bishops, and archbishops at ecumenical councils, placing them under excommunication for their faults. The Church alone is the pillar and ground of the truth.[6] She has the authority to interpret Holy Scripture, approve teachers, and glorify them.

Question: Are there many commandments of the Church?

Answer: Although there are many, the chief ones are nine: First, to worship daily in accordance with Christian custom, either

---

[1] Acts 16:4-5
[2] 1 Corinthians 3:11
[3] Ephesians 1:22
[4] Ephesians 5:23
[5] Matthew 18:17
[6] 1 Timothy 3:15

by listening attentively to the services in church or devoutly performing matins, hours, vespers, and compline. If possible, to attend the Holy Liturgy, especially on feast days and Sundays. A Christian who does not attend the Holy Liturgy on such days, being healthy and not traveling, especially when the church is nearby, commits a mortal sin. The devout person must always be in prayer, as it is written: *Pray without ceasing.*[1] And if there is any teaching, it should be heard with diligence, striving to live in a manner worthy of Christian life.

Question: What is the second commandment of the Church?

Answer: To observe the four fasts of the year according to Christian custom.[2] The first fast is before the Nativity of Christ, beginning on November 15. The second fast is the Great Fast, which the Lord Himself observed, as the Evangelist writes: *And when He had fasted forty days and forty nights, He was afterward an hungred.*[3] The third is the Apostles' Fast, beginning after the Sunday of All Saints, in memory of when the apostles, before going out to preach the Gospel, fasted and prayed to the Lord God for help, as Scripture testifies: *And when they had fasted and prayed, and laid their hands on them, they sent them away.*[4] So we too fast, praying that the Gospel, which the apostles preached, may continue to spread and bear fruit in the hearts of men. The fourth fast begins on the first of August and continues until the Dormition of the Most Holy God-bearer.

Question: Are there any other fasts?

Answer: Every week we are required to fast on Wednesdays and Fridays, according to Apostolic Canon 69. We are not to

---

[1] 1 Thessalonians 5:17
[2] Apostolic Canon 69
[3] Matthew 4:2
[4] Acts 13:3

fast on Saturdays and Sundays or on certain other appointed days, except for Great Saturday. We must also observe a fast on September 14 for the Exaltation of the Precious Cross, in remembrance of the voluntary Passion of Christ, for on that day the Gospel of His suffering is read. Similarly, we must fast on August 29, for the commemoration of the beheading of the holy prophet John the Baptist, and before the feasts of the Nativity of Christ and Theophany.

Question: What is the third commandment of the Church?

Answer: To hold priests in high and worthy honor as servants of God and our intercessors, especially one's spiritual father. Likewise, to honor those who labor in preaching the Word of God, as it is written: *Let the elders that rule well be counted worthy of double honor, especially they who labor in the word and doctrine.*[1]

Question: What is the fourth commandment of the Church?

Answer: To confess one's sins at least four times a year. Although it is more pious to do so more frequently, no one should go a whole year without confessing at least once. Such a person is under a curse and excommunication from the Church.

Question: What is the fifth commandment of the Church?

Answer: Not to read heretical books, nor to attend their assemblies, nor to listen to their teachings.[2] Also, those who are not learned should not engage in disputes with them, but should reject them in every way, according to the Scripture: *A man that is a heretic after the first and second admonition reject.*[3]

---

[1] 1 Timothy 5:17
[2] Apostolic Canon 64; Council of Laodicea, Canons 31, 32, 33, and 34
[3] Titus 3:10

Question: What is the sixth commandment of the Church?

Answer: To pray to the Lord God for all who are in authority, for the king, the senate, and for all the commonwealth, as well as for the spiritual authorities, especially for those who labor to spread the glory of God. The Apostle teaches us this, saying: *I exhort therefore, that, first of all, supplications, prayers, intercessions, and giving of thanks be made for all men; for kings, and for all that are in authority; that we may lead a quiet and peaceable life in all godliness and honesty. For this is good and acceptable in the sight of God our Savior, who will have all men to be saved, and to come unto the knowledge of the truth.*[1] We should also pray to God for the conversion of pagans, unbelievers, heretics, and apostates to the holy, true, and universal Church of Christ. Additionally, we must pray to the Lord to deliver all Christians from pagan captivity.

Question: What is the seventh commandment of the Church?

Answer: To observe fasts, prayers, almsgiving, and service to our brethren with the counsel and command of our spiritual leaders, with diligence. For this was the practice even in the days of the apostles, as Scripture testifies: *Peter therefore was kept in prison: but prayer was made without ceasing of the church unto God for him.*[2]

Question: What is the eighth commandment of the Church?

Answer: No one should take for their own use the things that are consecrated to the Church, whether they be immovable or movable. Likewise, clergy should not misuse them, but should distribute them for the needs of the Church and the poor. Above all, bishops should use church property for hospitality, schools,

---

[1] 1 Timothy 2:1-4
[2] Acts 12:5

ransoming captives, and caring for those in need, as Christians did in the days of the apostles. As the Scripture says: *Then the disciples, every man according to his ability, determined to send relief unto the brethren which dwelt in Judaea: which also they did, and sent it to the elders by the hands of Barnabas and Saul.*[1]

Question: What is the ninth commandment of the Church?

Answer: Not to marry on forbidden days,[2] and not to marry within prohibited degrees of kinship. Also, not to attend indecent spectacles or partake in inappropriate customs.

Question: What is the tenth article of faith?

Answer: *I acknowledge one baptism for the remission of sins.*

Question: What does this article teach?

Answer: Wherever baptism is mentioned, it gives us the form for understanding the holy mysteries of the Lord.

Question: What is a mystery (sacrament)?

Answer: A mystery is a visible thing, instituted by Christ,[3] which, when sanctified by the priest and administered to people, brings us invisible grace from the Lord God, sanctifying the person and helping them toward eternal life.

Question: How many things are understood in a mystery?

Answer: Four: the first is the true and visible thing itself, instituted by Christ. The second is the words by which the mystery receives its sanctification through the power of the Holy Ghost. The third is from whom we receive these mysteries. The

---

[1] Acts 11:29-30

[2] Basil the Great, To Amphilochius, Canon 27; Sixth Ecumenical Council, Canon 24

[3] Damascene, Book 4, Chapter 14

fourth is the action of the mystery.

Question: How many mysteries are there?

Answer: There are seven, corresponding to the gifts of the Holy Ghost, as confirmed by the holy catholic Church.

Question: What is the first mystery?

Answer: Baptism: which is the birth by water and the Spirit, and entrance into the Church of God, and thence to the kingdom of heaven, as it is written: *Verily, verily, I say unto thee, Except a man be born of water and of the Spirit, he cannot enter into the kingdom of God.*[1]

Question: What should be observed in this mystery?

Answer: The priests, who perform the mysteries, know this, as the church service books instruct them. The essential element is the water, natural and unchanged. In it, according to the order described in the church books, the priest, when baptizing, must say these words of Christ: *The servant of God is baptized in the name of the Father, and of the Son, and of the Holy Ghost.* These words, with the triple immersion, complete the baptism.

Question: What is the benefit of Holy Baptism?

Answer: When a person is immersed in water during baptism and washed, the original sin is invisibly washed away and cleansed from the soul, as the holy Apostle Paul teaches: *But ye are washed, but ye are sanctified, but ye are justified in the name of the Lord Jesus, and by the Spirit of our God.*[2] At that moment, we become members of Christ, and we are clothed in Him, according to the same Apostle Paul's teaching: *For as many*

---

[1] John 3:5
[2] 1 Corinthians 6:11; Gregory of Nyssa, On the Baptism of Christ

of you as have been baptized into Christ have put on Christ.[1] In this way, we become heirs of God and joint-heirs with Christ.[2]

Question: What is understood when someone approaches Holy Baptism?

Answer: It is fitting for anyone wishing to accept the Christian faith to confess it before their baptism, if they are of age, by themselves.[3] If it is an infant, then those who are present at the baptism and stand for them make promises on their behalf. It is important for the priest to know how best to administer the sacrament.

Question: What is the second mystery?

Answer: Chrismation, or the anointing with holy myrrh.[4] This is the confirmation of Holy Baptism, which strengthens and arms the baptized, making them an invincible warrior of Christ against the invisible enemy. After Chrismation, the Holy Ghost is received, as it was during the time of the apostles through the laying on of hands, as the Scripture testifies: *Then laid they their hands on them, and they received the Holy Ghost.*[5] Similarly, this anointing is now administered, as taught by the holy Apostle Paul: *Now He which stablisheth us with you in Christ, and hath anointed us, is God; who hath also sealed us, and given the earnest of the Spirit in our hearts.*[6]

Question: What should be known about the mystery of Chrismation?

---

[1] Galatians 3:27

[2] Romans 8:17

[3] Kyrian Service Book, Instruction for Catechumens II; Dionysius, On the Ecclesiastical Hierarchy, Chapter 2

[4] Dionysius, On the Ecclesiastical Hierarchy, Chapter 4

[5] Acts 8:17

[6] 2 Corinthians 1:21-22

Answer: First, the holy oil is consecrated by the greater bishops, from whom the priests receive it for this sacrament, following the prescribed custom. During the anointing, the priest should use the words: *The seal of the gift of the Holy Ghost.* This action should be performed on every baptized person, immediately after baptism, as the holy Church has united the sacraments of baptism and Chrismation together. Specific parts of the body are anointed, as described in the church service books.

Question: What is the third mystery?

Answer: The Mystery of the Lord's Supper, in which the true Body and Blood of Christ are present under the forms of bread and wine, in remembrance of Christ's Passion and for our eternal salvation.[1] It is sanctified and consumed, as the Apostle Paul teaches: *For as often as ye eat this bread, and drink this cup, ye do shew the Lord's death till He come.*[2] Our Savior also instructs us for our salvation: *Whoso eateth My flesh, and drinketh My blood, hath eternal life; and I will raise him up at the last day. For My flesh is meat indeed, and My blood is drink indeed.*[3]

Question: What should be observed in this mystery?

Answer: First, when the priest is preparing to perform the Holy Liturgy, it must be done with a pure mind and intention, following the order laid out by the holy Church, as set forth by the Church Fathers.[4] Additionally, the bread used must be pure leavened wheat, and the wine must be natural, slightly mixed with water. Other necessary elements must also be in place, as described in the service books.

---

[1] Damascene, Book 4, Chapter 9

[2] 1 Corinthians 11:26

[3] John 6:54-55

[4] Basil the Great, Chrysostom, and James in the Liturgy; Dionysius, On the Ecclesiastical Hierarchy, Chapter 3

Question: What is the benefit of the consecration and communion of this mystery?

Answer: The first benefit is in the consecration,[1] just as it is a bloodless sacrifice for the forgiveness of sins for the living, so too it benefits the dead. The second benefit is in communion, for Christ lives in us and we in Him, as it is written, *He that eateth My flesh, and drinketh My blood, dwelleth in Me, and I in him.*[2] The third benefit is that we inherit eternal life, as the Scripture also testifies: *He that eateth of this bread shall live forever.*[3] The fourth benefit is that we are freed from the temptations of demons because when they sense Christ dwelling within us, they cannot attack us. As this is explained in detail in the Great Catechism, every Christian should often and reverently attend the holy liturgy and partake of the Body and Blood of the Lord.[4]

Question: What is the fourth mystery?

Answer: Priesthood, which was established by Christ among the apostles.[5] Through the laying on of hands on the bishops, and from the bishops on the priests, they are consecrated by the church's order to administer the holy mysteries and teach the saving doctrine of Christ. As the Lord expressed in the following words, *Go ye therefore, and teach all nations, baptizing them in the name of the Father, and of the Son, and of the Holy Ghost.*[6] Similarly, the Apostle Paul also attests to this, saying, *Let a man so account of us, as of the ministers of Christ, and stewards of the mysteries of God.*[7] The priesthood encompasses these two main

---

[1] Chrysostom, Homilies on Genesis
[2] John 6:56
[3] John 6:58
[4] Chrysostom, Homily on 1 Timothy 4
[5] Chrysostom, On the Priesthood
[6] Matthew 28:19-20
[7] 1 Corinthians 4:1

offices and others subordinate to them. Therefore, it is necessary to know that no one who has not been ordained can be a minister of the sacraments, nor can anyone preach Christ's doctrine in the church without authorization, as it is written, *Wherefore I put thee in remembrance that thou stir up the gift of God, which is in thee by the putting on of my hands.*[1] For the laying on of hands is solely within the power of bishops.

Question: What else should be known about the mystery of priesthood?

Answer: It should be known that certain qualifications are required for a person to be consecrated to this mystery: First, the person must be whole and sound in body, without physical hindrance to the ministry, and must meet the age requirements as outlined in the rules. Second, the person must have the knowledge appropriate to the office. Third, the person's conscience should be free from guilt that would impede them from serving.

Question: What is the matter or form of the mystery of priesthood?

Answer: The matter is the laying on of the hands of the bishop on the head of the one receiving holy orders. The completion is achieved by the prayer recited by the bishop while laying on hands, during which he says, *The divine grace,* and so forth.

Question: What are the functions of this mystery?

Answer: As mentioned earlier, the functions are to administer the holy mysteries of the Lord and to teach the Holy Gospel.

Question: Are there any ranks before this mystery?

---

[1] 2 Timothy 1:6

Answer: There are ranks, which the bishops and priests know well. During the ordination, appropriate instruments for each rank are given to the ordinand according to church tradition.

Question: What is the fifth mystery?

Answer: Repentance, which is for the forgiveness of sins, with heartfelt contrition and the confession of sins, in hope of forgiveness, through the outpouring of the precious blood of the Son of God, and through the priestly absolution, for Christ gave the power to bind and loose.[1]

Question: What should be known about this mystery?

Answer: First, the penitent must be an Orthodox Christian believer, for without good faith, no repentance is effective. Second, only an Orthodox priest can absolve the penitent, for outside the Church, there is no salvation or absolution. Third, the one who approaches repentance should have sorrow and heartfelt contrition for the sins by which he has offended God and his neighbor. Fourth, all sins for which he repents must be confessed, for the priest cannot absolve what he does not know, as is testified in Holy Scripture, particularly in the Acts of the Apostles: *And many that believed came, and confessed, and shewed their deeds.*[2] Likewise, those who came to John the Baptist confessed their sins, as Mark the Evangelist testifies: *And there went out unto him all the land of Judaea, and they of Jerusalem, and were all baptized of him in the river of Jordan, confessing their sins.*[3] This is also confirmed by the apostolic command: *Confess your faults one to another.*[4] Therefore, we are

---

[1] Athanasius, On the Incarnation of God; Chrysostom, Homily 31 on Hebrews Chapter 12

[2] Acts 19:18

[3] Mark 1:5

[4] James 5:16

to confess only to those who have the authority to absolve and give counsel with knowledge.

Question: How is absolution of sins performed by the spiritual father?

Answer: After hearing the confession of the penitent, the priest thoroughly considers the sincerity of the confession, the contrition of the heart, and the commitment to a chaste life, and also the resolution to avoid sin. Based on the worthiness of the repentance, he absolves or retains sins. In absolving, he uses the following words in his prayers, saying, *By the authority given to me by Christ, I absolve you in the name of the Father, the Son, and the Holy Ghost*, making the person acceptable to receive the Body and Blood of the Lord, and ensuring that he will not be condemned on the Day of Judgment, according to the words: *Verily I say unto you, Whatsoever ye shall bind on earth shall be bound in heaven: and whatsoever ye shall loose on earth shall be loosed in heaven.*[1]

Question: What are the effects of this mystery?

Answer: The visible effects are that the person, freed from sin, gains a kind of second innocence, and from being a child of wrath and of disgrace, he becomes a child of the grace of God, once he has sufficiently atoned for his sins through repentance, according to the command and teaching of the spiritual father.[2]

Question: What is the sixth mystery?

Answer: The institution of marriage, which is entered by mutual consent from those who attain this estate without any corruption, and with the blessing of the priesthood: when they

---

[1] Matthew 18:18

[2] Chrysostom, Homily 5 on Psalm 142, On Repentance

pledge to each other to keep faith, honor, and marital love, it is established by prayer and blessing, and it is called a mystery, as it is written: *This is a great mystery.*[1] Such an institution of marriage is also praised by the Holy Scripture: *Marriage is honorable in all, and the bed undefiled*[2].[3]

Question: What benefits come from this mystery?

Answer: The first benefit is, that those who are not able to keep the purity of virginity may flee to marriage and avoid all fornication, as it is written, *Nevertheless, to avoid fornication, let every man have his own wife, and let every woman have her own husband.*[4] The second benefit is that children born of marriage are not only called honorable but are also holy. The third benefit is that in all circumstances and infirmities, especially the husband to the wife and the wife to the husband, they are closest, as the Holy Scripture teaches: *From the beginning of the creation God made them male and female. For this cause shall a man leave his father and mother, and cleave to his wife, and they twain shall be one flesh.*[5] The fourth benefit is that in the institution of marriage, those living in accordance with it will not receive any reproach from God or from men, nor will they suffer scruples in their conscience reproof.[6]

Question: What is the purpose of marriage?

Answer: The purpose of marriage is that the human race may multiply, and that the number of the appointed and elect in the

---

[1] Ephesians 5:32
[2] Hebrews 13:14
[3] Chrysostom, On Genesis, Homily 56
[4] 1 Corinthians 7:2
[5] Mark 10:6-8
[6] Chrysostom, Book 1 on Virginity

kingdom of heaven may be fulfilled.[1]

Question: What is the seventh mystery?

Answer: The anointing with oil for the sick, with prayers for the remission of sins and the healing of the body, as the Holy Scripture teaches: *They cast out many devils, and anointed with oil many that were sick, and healed them.*[2] And elsewhere: *Is any sick among you? Let him call for the elders of the church; and let them pray over him, anointing him with oil in the name of the Lord. And the prayer of faith shall save the sick, and the Lord shall raise him up; and if he have committed sins, they shall be forgiven him*[3].[4]

Question: What should be known about this mystery?

Answer: First, that the priests be of the Orthodox faith.[5] Second, that the thing used is proper, that is, oil, which was previously blessed by any priest. Third, that the sick person be of the Orthodox faith: and that before the anointing with oil, they confess. Fourth, that the prayer which is said over the sick person at the time of anointing represents the image of this mystery, saying: *Holy Father, healer of souls and bodies*, and so on.

Question: What is the effect or benefit of this mystery?

Answer: As mentioned above by St. James, so now I say, that there is remission of sins, and healing of the body.[6]

Question: What is the eleventh article?

---

[1] Genesis 1:28
[2] Mark 6:13
[3] James 5:14-15
[4] Basil the Great, To Amphilochius. Ch. 27, On The Holy Ghost
[5] Council of Carthage
[6] 1 Corinthians 11:30

Answer: *I await the resurrection of the dead.*

Question: How many things does this article teach?

Answer: Three: First, that it is certain and necessary that there will be a resurrection of human bodies from the dead, both of the good and the evil, as it is written: *Marvel not at this: for the hour is coming, in the which all that are in the graves shall hear his voice, and shall come forth; they that have done good, unto the resurrection of life; and they that have done evil, unto the resurrection of damnation.*[1]

Question: What or what kind of consolation is there in the kingdom of heaven?

Answer: There will be no bodily or temporal consolation there, according to the word of the Apostle. *For the kingdom of God is not meat and drink, but righteousness, and peace, and joy in the Holy Ghost.*[2] And elsewhere: *For in the resurrection they neither marry, nor are given in marriage, but are as the angels of God in heaven.*[3] Such consolation and joy will have no end in the kingdom of heaven.

Question: Will the soul and body have the same consolation, or not?

Answer: The soul, which together with the body in this present life has pleased God, will together with the body be glorified in the life to come. In glory, they will be like the angels, and they will shine like the sun, as it is written: *Then shall the righteous shine forth as the sun in the kingdom of their Father.*[4] Therefore, they will receive one and the same consolation and joy, together

---

[1] John 5:28-29
[2] Rom. 14:17
[3] Matt. 22:30
[4] Matt. 13:43

and indivisible. Amen.

Question: How should we understand the fate of the condemned?

Answer: They too will be cast into eternal fire with both soul and body, and there they will be tormented forever, as Christ has said: *Depart from me, ye cursed, into everlasting fire, prepared for the devil and his angels.*[1] And elsewhere: *Where their worm dieth not, and the fire is not quenched.*[2]

Question: Will the condemned ever come to the end of their torments?

Answer: By no means: For just as those in heaven, being incorruptible forever, will enjoy joy and consolation, so too those in hell, forever with both soul and body in the fire, will be tormented without end, and they shall never be consumed.[3]

---

[1] Matt. 25:41
[2] Mark 9:44
[3] Theophylact on Matthew 25

On Hope

Question: What is hope?

Answer: Hope is true and unwavering confidence in the Lord God, believing that with His assistance we will obtain eternal salvation.[1] And for all those things that we ask of the Lord God with faith, uniting them to His holy will, as the Holy Scripture teaches: *Cast not away therefore your confidence, which hath great recompense of reward.*[2] And elsewhere: *For we are saved by hope: but hope that is seen is not hope: for what a man seeth, why doth he yet hope for?*[3]

Question: In what does our hope consist?

Answer: Our hope is the Lord Jesus Christ Himself, as the holy Apostle Paul teaches, saying, *Paul, an apostle of Jesus Christ by the commandment of God our Savior, and Lord Jesus Christ, which is our hope.*[4] And this is to our glory, for in Him and through Him is eternal life, and all grace is given, as the Holy Scripture also says: *But ye, beloved, building up yourselves on your most holy faith, praying in the Holy Ghost, keep yourselves in the love of God, looking for the mercy of our Lord Jesus Christ unto eternal life.*[5]

Question: What is to be learned in hope?

---

[1] Basil the Great, Homily on Asceticism
[2] Hebrews 10:35
[3] Romans 8:24
[4] 1 Timothy 1:1
[5] Jude 1:20-21

Answer: Two things are to be learned: the Lord's Prayer and the Beatitudes.

Question: What is prayer?

Answer: Prayer is a request made with simplicity and faith to the Lord God, in hope of receiving what we ask for, or a glorification and thanksgiving to Him.

Question: How many parts is prayer divided into?

Answer: Into three parts: the first part, by which we glorify the Lord God for His majesty and glory. The second part, when we ask the Lord God for something. The third part is when we give thanks for the blessings we have already received from Him.

Question: What is the most well-known and exceptional prayer?

Answer: The Lord's Prayer, which Jesus Christ Himself taught His apostles, commanding them to pray in this way, saying: *After this manner therefore pray ye: Our Father which art in heaven,* and so on.[1]

Question: Into how many parts is the Lord's Prayer divided?

Answer: Into three parts: The first is the preface, in which we recognize to whom we are praying. The second part expresses the matter for which we ask or pray. The third part is the conclusion of the Lord's Prayer, in which there is an assurance that what we have asked, we shall receive, by the power and help of God.[2]

Question: What is the preface to the Lord's Prayer?

Answer: It is: *Our Father which art in heaven.*

---

[1] Matthew 6:9
[2] Theophylact, on Matthew 6

Question: What do I learn from this preface?

Answer: First, you learn that when you approach the Lord God in prayer, you must be well prepared in both thought and heart, as well as in conscience, so that this prayer may be pleasing before Him. Then, you understand that we are children of the Heavenly Father by grace. Therefore, when we ask, we ought to have great confidence toward Him. And as we are children of God, the Holy Scripture teaches us: *But as many as received him, to them gave he power to become the sons of God, even to them that believe on his name.*[1] And elsewhere: *And because ye are sons, God hath sent forth the Spirit of his Son into your hearts, crying, Abba, Father.*[2]

Question: What else do I learn from this?

Answer: We learn that we all have one Father, who, for our sake as His children, is ready to do all things for us, as Christ says: *For your heavenly Father knoweth that ye have need of all these things.*[3] And elsewhere: *And call no man your father upon the earth: for one is your Father, which is in heaven.*[4]

Question: What more does this preface teach?

Answer: It teaches that, having one Father, all the faithful and elect of God should confess themselves to be brethren, and pray for one another, according to the Scripture: *Pray for one another, that ye may be healed.*[5]

Question: How should I understand the phrase, *which art in heaven*?

---

[1] John 1:12
[2] Galatians 4:6
[3] Matthew 6:32
[4] Matthew 23:9
[5] James 5:16

Answer: The Lord and God is not only in heaven, but is everywhere and fills all things. However, He especially abides in heaven with greater grace and has His throne there, as it is said in the Psalms: *The Lord hath prepared his throne in the heavens; and his kingdom ruleth over all.*[1]

Question: In the second part of the prayer, how many petitions are there?

Answer: Seven: the first is, *Hallowed be Thy name.*

Question: What does this petition include?

Answer: First, we ask and pray to the Lord God to grant us to live in piety, to live according to His will and good pleasure, so that His holy name may be glorified, as He Himself teaches: *Let your light so shine before men, that they may see your good works, and glorify your Father which is in heaven.*[2]

Question: What else do I learn from this petition?

Answer: You learn this, that you should never commit any evil or deceit by which the name of God might be blasphemed, so that it may not be said of you, as it is written: *For the name of God is blasphemed among the Gentiles through you.*[3] And elsewhere: *They profess that they know God; but in works they deny him*[4].[5]

Question: What is the second petition?

Answer: *Thy kingdom come.*

---

[1] Psalm 102
[2] Matthew 5:16; Chrysostom, on Matthew 6 Homily 20; Theophylact, on the same
[3] Romans 2:24
[4] Titus 1:16
[5] Gregory of Nyssa in Homily 8 on the Lord's Prayer

Question: What does this petition include?

Answer: First, we ask and pray that the Lord God may come into our hearts and dwell there by His grace and mercy, so that we may have righteousness, peace, and joy, and that sin may no longer reign in our hearts and bodies, according to the Apostle's teaching: *Let not sin therefore reign in your mortal body, that ye should obey it in the lusts thereof. Neither yield ye your members as instruments of unrighteousness unto sin: but yield yourselves unto God, as those that are alive from the dead, and your members as instruments of righteousness unto God.*[1]

Question: What is the second thing contained in this petition?

Answer: We confess this: that, having a good conscience, we fervently pray to the Lord God that He may grant us a Christian departure from this body, and to always be with Him, as the Apostle Paul says of himself: *Having a desire to depart, and to be with Christ; which is far better.*[2] We also pray that the number of God's elect may be fulfilled, and that the coming of Christ may be hastened, along with the resurrection of the dead. And that the enemy of our souls may no longer reign in this world, but that God may be all in all.[3]

Question: What is the third petition?

Answer: *Thy will be done on earth, as it is in heaven.*

Question: What does this petition include?

Answer: In this petition, we first ask the Lord God, that He may grant us to know His holy will, which is revealed in His holy commandments and in all the teachings of Christ the Lord, as

---

[1] Romans 6:12–13
[2] Philippians 1:23
[3] 1 Corinthians 15:28

described in the Gospel. And once we know His will, that we may fulfill it with His help, according to our strength, as Christ Himself teaches: *He that hath my commandments, and keepeth them, he it is that loveth me: and he that loveth me shall be loved of my Father, and I will love him, and will manifest myself to him*[1].[2]

Question: What is the second thing I should learn from this petition?

Answer: In this petition, we pray to the Lord God that, just as the angels in heaven fulfill the will of God in all things and glorify Him in perfect unity, so also Christians on earth, in love and unity, with one mouth and one heart, may glorify the Lord God and fulfill His holy will, for which the Orthodox Church prays to the Lord God every day.

Question: What is the fourth petition?

Answer: *Give us this day our daily bread.*

Question: What does this petition include?

Answer: In this petition, we first ask and pray to the Lord God to give us the bread by which the human soul lives, that is, the hearing of the word of God, concerning which Christ Himself says: *Man shall not live by bread alone, but by every word that proceedeth out of the mouth of God.*[3] Then we ask for the other bread by which the soul lives, that we may worthily partake of the body and blood of Christ, for our eternal salvation. This bread our Savior Christ Himself calls His own body: *I am the living bread which came down from heaven: if any man eat of this bread, he shall live forever: and the bread that I will give is*

---

[1] John 14:21

[2] Theophylact on Matthew 5:48

[3] Matthew 4:4; Gregory of Nyssa, Homily 4 on the Lord's Prayer; Chrysostom and Theophylact on the appointed readings

my flesh, which I will give for the life of the world.[1]

Question: What else should I learn from this petition?

Answer: We also pray for this daily bread, that God may grant us to enjoy it in peace, and together with the bread, for all other necessities without which a person cannot live, but not in excess. By the word *this day*, He distances us from excessive care for future material things, as He teaches elsewhere, saying: *Take therefore no thought for the morrow: for the morrow shall take thought for the things of itself. Sufficient unto the day is the evil thereof.*[2]

Question: What is the fifth petition?

Answer: *And forgive us our debts, as we forgive our debtors.*

Question: What is included in this petition?

Answer: First, in this petition we ask that God may forgive all the sins we have committed after our holy baptism, just as we forgive our debtors, according to the word of Christ: *For if ye forgive men their trespasses, your heavenly Father will also forgive you: but if ye forgive not men their trespasses, neither will your Father forgive your trespasses*[3].[4]

Question: What is the sixth petition?

Answer: *And lead us not into temptation.*

Question: What is included in this petition?

Answer: First, in this petition we ask the Lord, that when the enemy wages war against us with fleshly and worldly lusts, He

---

[1] John 6:51
[2] Matthew 6:34
[3] Matthew 6:14-15
[4] Gregory of Nyssa, Homily 5 on the Lord's Prayer

may unfailingly help us with His holy grace, for without Him we can do nothing, as He Himself says: *For without me ye can do nothing.*[1] For, in our weakness, the power of Christ is glorified, as He said to the Apostle Paul: *My grace is sufficient for thee: for my strength is made perfect in weakness*[2].[3]

Question: What is the second thing we ask of the Lord God in this petition?

Answer: We ask, that He may humble the hearts of all the enemies and persecutors of Christ's Church, and deliver us from our persecutors and from their malicious schemes devised by the devil. And if we happen to fall into temptations, may He not allow us to be tempted beyond our strength, as it is written: *God is faithful, who will not suffer you to be tempted above that ye are able; but will with the temptation also make a way to escape, that ye may be able to bear it*[4].[5]

Question: What is the seventh petition?

Answer: *But deliver us from the evil one.*

Question: What is included in this petition?

Answer: In this petition, we ask and pray to the Lord God, that He may protect us from Satan, who is the originator of all evil, along with wicked people. Here, we also ask that He grant us correction in life, that we may cease from sin, and that He remove from us the punishment prepared for our sins, both temporal and eternal.[6]

---

[1] John 15:5
[2] 2 Corinthians 12:9
[3] Gregory of Nyssa, Homily 5 on the Lord's Prayer
[4] 1 Corinthians 10:13
[5] Theophylact on Matthew 6
[6] Chrysostom on Matthew 6:12; Gregory of Nyssa, Homily 5 on the

Question: What is the third part of the Lord's Prayer?

Answer: The conclusion: *For Thine is the kingdom, and the power, and the glory, for ever. Amen.*

Question: What is included in these words?

Answer: These words, spoken at the end of this prayer, were taught by Christ Himself in the Gospel of Matthew, and they include this declaration: that whatever we ask according to God's will, He can accomplish for us, because His power and dominion extend over all the world. And this is not so much for our sake, as sinful people, but for the sake of His own holy glory. Therefore, we are instructed to ask according to His holy will, as St. John teaches us, saying: *And this is the confidence that we have in Him, that, if we ask anything according to His will, He heareth us.*[1] The word *Amen* is placed at the end for the same reason, to signify that this is so, and not otherwise.[2]

Question: How many Beatitudes are there?

Answer: Christ enumerates nine Beatitudes in the Gospel of Matthew,[3] as Chrysostom also explains: *Moses gave ten commandments in righteousness, but Jesus the Lord gave nine Beatitudes.*[4]

Question: What is the first Beatitude?

Answer: *Blessed are the poor in spirit, for theirs is the kingdom of heaven.*[5]

Lord's Prayer

[1] 1 John 5:14
[2] Chrysostom on Matthew 6, Homily 15
[3] Matthew 5:3-12
[4] Chrysostom on Matthew 5, Homily 15; Theophylact on the same
[5] Chrysostom on 1 Corinthians 15; Chrysostom on Matthew 5, Homily 15

Question: What should I learn from this Beatitude?

Answer: You learn that voluntary poverty, which is found through the free choice of the human heart, truly makes a person both poor and blessed. This is greater than wealth, for in poverty, wealth does not hinder one's love for God and neighbor, as it was with the first Christians: they sold their possessions and laid the money at the apostles' feet for the benefit of the poor and needy brethren: *Neither said any of them that ought of the things which he possessed was his own; but they had all things common.*[1]

Question: What is the second Beatitude?

Answer: *Blessed are they that mourn, for they shall be comforted.*

Question: What should I learn from this Beatitude?

Answer: You learn this: those who truly mourn are those who, in this world, weep for their own sins and for the sins of their neighbors. Likewise, those who suffer wrongs from the more powerful mourn, such as widows, orphans, and poor people, and those who are unaware of how to defend themselves. Those who mourn, and those who grieve in slavery to pagans, and those who endure persecution for the sake of the Christian faith: they are blessed in this world, having spiritual consolation, and in the world to come, they will have true comfort in heaven.[2]

Question: What is the third Beatitude?

Answer: *Blessed are the meek, for they shall inherit the earth.*

Question: What should I learn from this Beatitude?

Answer: You should learn that the meek are those who think

---

[1]Acts 4:34-35

[2]Chrysostom on Matthew 5, Homily 15; Theophylact on the same; Gregory of Nyssa, Homily 3 on the Beatitudes

humbly of themselves and do not exalt themselves above others in body, wealth, wisdom, or life, but always apply to themselves the words of Christ: *When ye shall have done all those things which are commanded you, say, We are unprofitable servants: we have done that which was our duty to do.*[1]

Question: What is the fourth Beatitude?

Answer: *Blessed are they which do hunger and thirst after righteousness, for they shall be filled.*

Question: What should I learn from this Beatitude?

Answer: You should learn that those who are truly blessed are those who, in justice, seek to practice righteousness. Likewise, blessed are those who are unjustly condemned and reproached, who patiently endure this for the sake of God. Here, judges and rulers should learn to render justice to all if they wish to be blessed, remembering the words of the Psalm: *Judge the fatherless and the oppressed, that the man of the earth may no more oppress.*[2] Those who always hunger for righteousness, even if they cannot obtain it, should not lose hope, knowing the prophetic words: *For the needy shall not always be forgotten: the expectation of the poor shall not perish for ever.*[3] For when they see the face of God, they will be filled with righteousness when His glory is revealed.

Question: What is the fifth Beatitude?

Answer: *Blessed are the merciful, for they shall obtain mercy.*

Question: What are the works of mercy?

Answer: The works of mercy are twofold: some are of the body,

---

[1] Gregory of Nyssa, Homily 12 on the Beatitudes
[2] Psalm 9:19
[3] Psalm 9:18

and others are of the soul.[1]

Question: What are the corporal (physical) works of mercy?

Answer: There are seven: which Christ Himself will enumerate on the Day of Judgment: to feed the hungry, to give drink to the thirsty, to clothe the naked, to visit and comfort those in prison, to visit the sick and advise them concerning their salvation and physical health, to take in the stranger or those who have no place to lay their heads, and to shelter and care for them as best as one can according to their condition. To these six virtues should also be added that we gladly receive into our homes those who are on pilgrimage to holy places, and we should not abandon the poor and needy lying in the streets, but take them into our homes and serve them for the salvation of our souls. The seventh corporal work of mercy, as the Holy Scripture commands in Tobit, is to bury the dead, especially those who have left nothing behind for their burial. And while burying them, we should pray to the Lord God for the forgiveness of their sins. For as the angel Raphael said to Tobit, *When thou didst pray with tears, and didst bury the dead, and didst leave thy dinner, and hide the dead by day in thy house, and bury them by night, I did bring thy prayers to the Lord.*[2]

Question: What are the spiritual works of mercy?

Answer: There are also seven: first, to lead a sinner away from sin, as the Holy Scripture teaches: *Brethren, if any of you do err from the truth, and one convert him; let him know, that he which converteth the sinner from the error of his way shall save a soul from death, and shall hide a multitude of sins.*[3]

---

[1] Theophylact on Matthew 25
[2] Tobit 12:12-13
[3] James 5:19-20

78

Question: What is the second spiritual work of mercy?

Answer: To teach the ignorant, first, the will and law of God, how they should live according to the Christian faith, and then how to pray to God. Third, in whatever pertains to a good life, whatever you know, teach your neighbor without envy, lest you be condemned like the one who received only one talent.[1]

Question: What is the third spiritual work of mercy?

Answer: To give sound advice to those in need of counsel, whether to lead them from error to the right path or in all virtues, as mentioned above concerning the gifts of the Holy Ghost.

Question: What is the fourth spiritual work of mercy?

Answer: To ask and pray to the Lord God for all those in authority, and for those who desire to receive God's grace and mercy, as you may find more fully explained in the commandments of the Church.

Question: What is the fifth spiritual work of mercy?

Answer: To comfort those who mourn or are sorrowful, not only with kind words, but also with deeds.

Question: What is the sixth spiritual work of mercy?

Answer: Not to allow injustice to be done, and to prevent the faithful from being deceived by heretics. One should strive in every way to seek and bring back anyone who is not in the Orthodox faith.

Question: What is the seventh spiritual work of mercy?

Answer: To patiently endure any wrongs inflicted upon us, from anyone and in any way, with joy, and to overlook them,

---

[1]Matthew 25:24-30

so that the Lord God may also overlook our sins. All these works of mercy should be done with great diligence and zeal, for the greater reward from God.

Question: What is the sixth Beatitude?

Answer: *Blessed are the pure in heart, for they shall see God.*

Question: What should I learn from this Beatitude?

Answer: Blessed are those who maintain purity in all virtues, not only bodily purity but also purity of heart, striving even in thought to avoid all impurity, by which even marriage is kept undefiled.[1]

Question: What is the seventh Beatitude?

Answer: *Blessed are the peacemakers, for they shall be called the sons of God.*

Question: What should I learn about this Beatitude?

Answer: First, the primary partakers of this Beatitude are the priests, who reconcile God with man through the bloodless sacrifice. Likewise, the pious laypeople who make God merciful through their prayers, interceding for their neighbors, are blessed also. Blessed also are those who make peace among people, stepping in to intercede so that Christian blood is not shed in vain.

Question: What is the eighth Beatitude?

Answer: *Blessed are they which are persecuted for righteousness' sake, for theirs is the kingdom of heaven.*

Question: What should I learn from this Beatitude?

---

[1]Theophylact on Matthew 5; Gregory of Nyssa, Homily 5 on the Beatitudes

Answer: This Beatitude includes all those who speak the truth and suffer persecution from men, such as teachers, judges, and rulers, when they speak righteousness and endure malice from people because of it.

Question: What is the ninth Beatitude?

Answer: *Blessed are ye when men shall revile you, and persecute you, and shall say all manner of evil against you falsely, for my sake. Rejoice, and be exceeding glad, for great is your reward in heaven.*

Question: What should I learn from this Beatitude?

Answer: This Beatitude applies to the martyrs and to all who endure persecution when anyone hinders their piety, takes away their churches, possessions, and freedom, drives them from their positions and cities, or even, in some cases, delivers them to death for the sake of the faith.

On Love for God and Neighbor

Question: What is the teaching of the third part?

Answer: It is the teaching of love for God and neighbor, for on these two commandments the whole law is founded,[1] as Christ teaches, saying: *On these two commandments hang all the law and the prophets.*[2]

Question: On which commandments is love for God and neighbor built?

Answer: On the commandments given by God to Moses on the two tablets. On the first tablet are four commandments of God, which teach how we must love the Lord our God and relate to Him. On the second tablet are six commandments, which teach how we must love our neighbor as ourselves and behave toward him.

Question: What should be learned from these commandments?

Answer: First, you should know that some commandments instruct us to do good, while others forbid us to do evil. And if someone does good and refrains from evil, such a person keeps God's commandments.

Question: What happens when someone fulfills God's commandments?

---

[1]Chrysostom on Psalm 140
[2]Matthew 22:40

Answer: The fulfillment of the commandments is the fruit of Christian faith, according to the Savior's teaching: *Ye shall know them by their fruits. Do men gather grapes of thorns, or figs of thistles?*[1] And elsewhere: *By this shall all men know that ye are my disciples, if ye have love one to another.*[2]

Question: What happens when someone does not keep God's commandments?

Answer: Sin arises from this, and from sin comes death, according to the Apostle's teaching: *Wherefore, as by one man sin entered into the world, and death by sin; and so death passed upon all men, for that all have sinned.*[3]

Question: Are God's commandments Christian virtues, or temptations to sin?

Answer: Indeed, they are truly virtues, for if someone always meditates on God's commandments, that person lives virtuously in the world. But whoever disregards God's commandments sins.

Question: What are the first Christian virtues?

Answer: The first Christian virtues are three, without which no one can be saved. They are called theological virtues: faith, hope, and love.[4]

Question: From these virtues, which other virtues arise first?

Answer: Two[5] other virtues of Christian piety arise: prayer

---

[1] Matthew 7:16-17
[2] John 13:35
[3] Romans 5:12
[4] 1 Corinthians 13:13
[5] Here the text says "Three", which is clearly a mistake, as only two virtues are listed

and acts of mercy, about which we have already learned in their appropriate places.

Question: From these virtues, what other virtues proceed?

Answer: Four cardinal virtues: wisdom, justice, courage, and temperance.[1]

Question: How should I understand Christian wisdom?

Answer: You should know that Christian wisdom is the knowledge of God's will, by which we should live in the world, as the holy Apostle Paul teaches: *Be ye not unwise, but understanding what the will of the Lord is.*[2] Along with this wisdom comes true and sincere integrity, about which Christ Himself says: *Be ye therefore wise as serpents, and harmless as doves.*[3]

Question: How should I understand Christian justice?

Answer: Christian justice is not only about loving those who love us, but even if someone does evil to us, we must not seek revenge. And not only must we not seek revenge, but we are also obliged to pray to God for them.

Question: How should I understand temperance?

Answer: Temperance is the maintaining of moderation in all Christian ways, according to the Apostle's teaching: *Let us walk honestly, as in the day; not in rioting and drunkenness, not in chambering and wantonness, not in strife and envying. But put ye on the Lord Jesus Christ, and make not provision for the flesh, to fulfill the lusts thereof.*[4]

---

[1] Gregory of Nyssa on Ecclesiastes, Homily 6
[2] Ephesians 5:17
[3] Matthew 10:16
[4] Romans 13:13-14

Question: How should I understand courage?

Answer: We have already learned about courage in the section on the gifts of the Holy Ghost. Read it there.[1]

Question: What is sin?

Answer: Sin is nothing other than the transgression of God's law and will, from which death is born.[2]

Question: Into how many types is sin divided? **Answer:** One type is mortal sin, and another is everyday sin, as St. John the Theologian teaches: *There is a sin unto death, and there is a sin not unto death.*[3]

Question: What is mortal sin?

Answer: Mortal sin is the transgression against God or one's neighbor, by which we fall away from God's grace, do not repent, and die in it, thereby dying eternally. For this reason, it is called a mortal sin.

Question: Into how many parts are mortal sins divided?

Answer: Into three parts: in the first part are the mortal sins that are the gravest; in the second part are sins against the Holy Ghost; and in the third part are sins that cry out to God for vengeance.

Question: How many are the grave mortal sins?

Answer: Seven: 1. Gluttony, 2. Fornication, 3. Greed, 4. Wrath, 5. Sloth, 6. Vainglory, 7. Pride.

Question: What are the sins against the Holy Ghost?

---

[1] Above, page 46
[2] Romans 3:23
[3] 1 John 5:16-17

Answer: First, if someone, seeing God's abundant grace upon themselves, boldly continues in sin. Second, despairing of God's mercy. Third, resisting the evident and known truth.[1] Likewise, causing discord among brethren.

Question: What are the sins that cry out to God for vengeance?

Answer: First, willful murder; second, the sin of Sodom; third, oppressing widows and orphans; fourth, withholding the wages of laborers.[2] Also included are dishonoring parents and benefactors.

Question: What is an everyday (or daily) sin?

Answer: It is the transgression of God's will and commandments by which we daily offend God and our neighbor. However, it does not cause God's grace to depart from us, for we quickly reflect on it and repent. These sins are without number.

Question: Can a person partake in the sins of others?

Answer: Yes, when someone who could lead another away from sin does not do so. Likewise, if someone does not punish, though they have the power to punish—such as a master over his servant, a father over his son, or a husband over his wife—or any ruler over their subordinates. In the same way, if someone gives another person encouragement to sin in any manner, they become a participant in that sin.

Question: What is the first commandment of the first tablet of God's commandments?

Answer: It is this: *I am the Lord thy God, which have brought thee out of the land of Egypt, out of the house of bondage. Thou*

---

[1]Genesis 4:7

[2]Psalm 145:9; Psalm 36:21

shalt have no other gods before me.[1]

Question: How should I understand this commandment?

Answer: You should understand that the Lord God, the Creator of heaven and earth, who besides Himself has no equal, revealed Himself to the Jewish people and commanded them not to have any other gods, reminding them of the blessing that He brought them out of Egyptian bondage. We Christians, likewise, are obliged to confess, glorify, and obey this one true God, as the Apostle Paul teaches: *Giving thanks unto the Father, which hath made us meet to be partakers of the inheritance of the saints in light: who hath delivered us from the power of darkness, and hath translated us into the kingdom of His dear Son: in whom we have redemption through His blood, even the forgiveness of sins.*[2]

Question: Who transgresses this commandment?

Answer: First, those who say there is no God, as the Psalm says: *The fool hath said in his heart, there is no God.*[3] Second, those who believe in many gods, as the unbelieving nations do. Third, those who submit to the invisible enemy, such as sorcerers, magicians, and all who practice witchcraft and serve demons. Alongside them are all heretics who wrongly believe about the one God in the Holy Trinity.[4] In addition, those who place more hope in prosperity, wisdom, learning, treasures, bodily beauty, or even in themselves more than in God.

Question: How should I understand the invocation of the saints in this context?

Answer: The invocation of the saints increases the glory of the

---

[1] Exodus 20:2-3
[2] Colossians 1:12-14
[3] Psalm 13:1; John of Damascus, Book 4, Chapter 3
[4] Philippians 3:18

true God and is therefore not contrary to this commandment. For when we ask the saints to intercede with God, we first acknowledge the grace they have received from God and seek to partake of it ourselves, primarily through the merits of Christ's precious blood, and secondarily through the prayers of all the saints.[1]

Question: For what reason do we invoke all the saints for help?

Answer: First, because we, due to our sins, dare not approach God directly, so we present them as our intercessors, for they, being already in His unchanging grace, assist us.[2] Second, because they pray for us as for their brethren. Third, just as in heaven the lesser angels approach God through the greater ones, so we approach God through the saints, asking for mercy and grace, praying through the greater to the lesser, and through the nearer to God.[3]

Question: Teach me from the Holy Scriptures about the invocation of the saints.

Answer: If the saints ask God for vengeance upon the wicked, as we have testimony in the Revelation of John, saying: *And they cried with a loud voice, saying, How long, O Lord, holy and true, dost Thou not judge and avenge our blood on them that dwell on the earth?*[4] then much more do their intercessions and prayers to God bring us blessings.

Question: Do the saints know of our prayers and needs?

---

[1] Matthew 10:32; John of Damascus, Book 4, Chapter 16; John 16:23; Romans 3:30

[2] John of Damascus, Book 4, Chapter 16

[3] John of Damascus, Book 4, Chapter 16; Dionysius, On the Celestial Hierarchy, Chapter 15

[4] Revelation 6:10; John of Damascus, Book 4, Chapter 17; Prayers for the Dead

Answer: The souls of the saints who have departed from this world, though by their nature they may not know of our infirmities, by the grace given to them by God, by which they are made like the angels, they know all our deeds and needs. They bring our prayers, alms, and other good deeds before the throne of God, especially since, while living in this world and enduring many hindrances, they knew and understood by God's grace what each person needed. Much more now, being in greater grace and unchanging glory, they know our needs and intercede for us before the Lord God as His faithful servants and close friends, as you will find more extensively explained in the Great Catechism.

Question: What is the second commandment?

Answer: *Thou shalt not make unto thee any graven image, or any likeness of anything that is in heaven above, or that is in the earth beneath, or that is in the waters under the earth: thou shalt not bow down thyself to them, nor serve them: for I the Lord thy God am a jealous God, visiting the iniquity of the fathers upon the children unto the third and fourth generation of them that hate Me, and shewing mercy unto thousands of them that love Me, and keep My commandments.*[1]

Question: How should I understand this commandment?

Answer: In this commandment, the Lord God commands not to make idols, which the pagans honored and gave therein the glory due to God. These were false and deceitful gods, for in those times the Jews were prone to idolatry.

Question: How should I understand the icons that the Orthodox Church possesses?

---

[1] Exodus 20:4-6

Answer: Icons are not idols of false and deceitful gods, but they are images of our Savior Jesus Christ, the true God, according to His assumed human nature, as well as of the most pure Virgin God-bearer and of all the saints. Just as in the Old Testament the cherubim, which were in the temple of the Lord, were not forbidden, because they were not contrary to God's will and glory, so too the images that the Orthodox Church holds are not contrary to this commandment. For everything written in the Gospel and in other Holy Scriptures, regarding God's chosen servants and beloved friends, is presented to us in their images, so that we may strive to inherit their virtues and piety.[1]

Question: How should I understand the relics of the saints and their bodies?

Answer: The bodies of the saints, during their lifetime, were filled with the grace and gift of the Holy Ghost, and therefore, even after death, the Lord God is glorified and magnified in their bodies, performing great and unspeakable miracles: *God is wonderful in His saints.*[2] If anyone does not believe, let them go and see where the relics of the saints are, and that the invisible enemy especially recognizes their power and fears them.[3]

Question: What is the third commandment?

Answer: *Thou shalt not take the name of the Lord thy God in vain, for the Lord will not hold him guiltless that taketh His name in vain.*[4]

---

[1] John of Damascus, Prayer 1, 2, 3; Gregory of Nyssa, Homily 2, Sermon 2; Basil, Homily 18 to Amphilochius on the Holy Ghost; Eusebius, Book 1, Church History

[2] Psalm 67:36

[3] John of Damascus, Book 4, Chapter 16

[4] Exodus 20:7

Question: How should I understand this commandment?

Answer: First, you should learn from this commandment not to take the name of the Lord your God in vain, meaning not to swear falsely or argue dishonestly, deceiving others with lies. For this will not go without God's judgment upon you. Second, you should not use God's name in jest or mockery, but whenever you mention the Lord God, do so with honor and reverence, remembering Him as your Lord and Creator.[1] Furthermore, any promise made to the Lord God must be kept, for it is better not to vow to the Lord God than to vow and fail to fulfill it.[2] Moreover, not only does the one who swears falsely transgress this commandment, but also the one who unjustly leads someone else to swear. This commandment also applies to those who, for the sake of worldly vanity, forsake the Orthodox Catholic faith promised at holy baptism. For God's judgment is upon them and their household in this world temporarily, and in the world to come, eternally.

Question: What is the fourth commandment?

Answer: *Remember the sabbath day, to keep it holy. Six days shalt thou labor, and do all thy work: but the seventh day is the sabbath of the Lord thy God: in it thou shalt not do any work, thou, nor thy son, nor thy daughter, thy manservant, nor thy maidservant, nor thy cattle, nor thy stranger that is within thy gates: for in six days the Lord made heaven and earth, the sea, and all that in them is, and rested the seventh day: wherefore the Lord blessed the sabbath day, and hallowed it.*[3]

Question: What should I learn from this commandment?

---

[1] Psalm 71
[2] Psalm 75
[3] Exodus 20:8-11

Answer: First, you should learn that all those days in which the Lord God showed special blessings to mankind are worthy of being honored and remembered, setting aside all other distractions, and devoting the day solely to the glorification and thanksgiving to the Lord God. This day was the Sabbath under the Old Law, symbolizing God's rest. However, under the New Grace, the Lord's Day (Sunday) has replaced it, as a symbol of the redemption and renewal through the resurrection of the Son of God from the dead. On this day, nothing else should be done but glorifying God and remembering His blessings. The same understanding applies to other feasts of the Lord, in which particular blessings are remembered and celebrated according to the commandments of the Church.

Question: What is the fifth commandment, the first of the second tablet?

Answer: *Honor thy father and thy mother: that thy days may be long upon the land which the Lord thy God giveth thee.*[1]

Question: How should I understand this commandment?

Answer: This commandment is the first among those that concern our neighbor. Among our neighbors, our parents are first in love and honor, and thus the Lord God commands that we hold them in appropriate honor and love, for, after the Lord God, they have bestowed upon us the greatest blessings. Under the term "parents," we should also understand all our benefactors, such as teachers, masters, and those in positions of authority, as well as anyone who does us good, according to the teaching of the Apostle Paul: *Let every soul be subject unto the higher powers. For there is no power but of God.*[2]

---

[1] Exodus 20:12

[2] Romans 13:1

Question: What is the sixth commandment?

Answer: *Thou shalt not kill.*[1]

Question: How should I understand this commandment?

Answer: This commandment forbids any form of unlawful killing, whether of the body or of the soul through scandal. However, when judges lawfully administer punishment, they do not sin but rather increase justice.

Question: What is the seventh commandment?

Answer: *Thou shalt not commit adultery.*[2]

Question: How should I understand this commandment?

Answer: This commandment instructs people to abstain from adultery, and Christ commands even more perfectly not to commit adultery even by lustful looks. There is also spiritual adultery, committed by those who fall away from the Orthodox Catholic Faith. Similarly, those who vow to live in monastic purity, poverty, and obedience but break their vow are also committing adultery.

Question: What is the eighth commandment?

Answer: *Thou shalt not steal.*[3]

Question: What should I learn from this commandment?

Answer: You should learn not to take anything that belongs to another, whether in secret or openly, through deceit or fraud in positions of authority and service. This is all prohibited by the Lord in this commandment. As the Apostle Paul clearly teaches:

---

[1] Exodus 20:13
[2] Exodus 20:14
[3] Exodus 20:15

Know ye not that the unrighteous shall not inherit the kingdom of God? Be not deceived: neither fornicators, nor idolaters, nor adulterers, nor effeminate, nor abusers of themselves with mankind, nor thieves, nor covetous, nor drunkards, nor revilers, nor extortioners, shall inherit the kingdom of God.[1] This also applies to usurers.

Question: What is the ninth commandment?

Answer: *Thou shalt not bear false witness against thy neighbor.*[2]

Question: What should I learn from this commandment?

Answer: We must not knowingly bear false witness against anyone, for this is contrary to both God and neighbor. Similarly, we should not give or accept false testimony even against our worst enemy in court, for we must not do evil in place of good.

Question: What is the tenth commandment?

Answer: *Thou shalt not covet thy neighbor's wife, thou shalt not covet thy neighbor's house, his field, nor his manservant, nor his maidservant, nor his ox, nor his ass, nor anything that is thy neighbor's.*[3]

Question: How should I understand this commandment?

Answer: This commandment is the most perfect, and Christ also proclaimed it when He commanded not only to refrain from the act itself but to root out even the thought of desiring anything that belongs to your neighbor. If someone keeps this commandment, they will truly live in love with their neighbor. In the world to come, they will inherit the kingdom of heaven

---

[1] 1 Corinthians 6:9-10
[2] Exodus 20:16
[3] Exodus 20:17

with all the saints; Amen.

From St. Gennady, Patriarch of Constantinople.

On Faith

Since holding the Orthodox faith is the foundation of good works, the word shall begin with faith.

Chapter 1. Believe in the Father, and the Son, and the Holy Ghost, the undivided and unconfused Trinity, one Godhead. The Father is unbegotten, the Son is begotten, but not created, the Holy Ghost is neither begotten nor created, but proceeding. Three in one will, one glory, one honor, and one worship, received from all creation—angels and humans alike—eternal and everlasting, and abiding forever.

Chapter 2. Believe in the incarnation of the Son of God as truly real, not a mere appearance, in two natures—Divinity and humanity. He is fully God in His divinity and fully man in His incarnation, perfect in both.

Chapter 3. Call His mother, who gave birth to Him, the God-bearer,[1] the Virgin and Mother, and believe that she gave birth to Christ and nourished Him. As a virgin, she remained a virgin even after giving birth.

Chapter 4. Worship[2] the Cross of Christ with faith, for on it the Lord accomplished salvation for all mankind.

Chapter 5. Honor the icon of Christ, of His most pure Mother, and of all His saints with faith, as if speaking lovingly to them in prayer. Christ, the meek Lamb, Emmanuel, was led to sacrifice, freely going to the slaughter. Come, sing, and worship the eternal life who was hung on the Cross.

Chapter 6. Pray to all the saints who have pleased the Lord, as they are helpers and intercessors for those who come to them, since they have gained confidence before God as faithful servants

---

[1] Θεοτόκος, Богородица

[2] That is, to make obeisance, or to bow down before

to their Master.

Chapter 7. Kiss the relics of the saints with faith and give them honor, for they suffered for the sake of Christ.

Chapter 8. Believe in the mysteries of God, in the body and blood of Christ, and partake with fear, that you may become a participant in His heavenly kingdom.

Chapter 9. Reject unbelief and do not say, "How can bread be the body and wine the blood?" but understand that nothing is impossible for God, though impossible for man.

Chapter 10. Believe in the resurrection of the dead and in the life of the world to come, according to the inexpressible word of the Lord, which you hear in the teaching of the Gospel.

Chapter 11. Remember the judgment, expect to give an answer, and the recompense according to deeds, believe that it will come, and it shall come.

Chapter 12. Love the Lord your God with all your heart and strength, and direct all your deeds and conduct to pleasing Him.

Chapter 13. Likewise, love your neighbor, with whom you were born in the same baptismal font, meaning every Christian, especially your brother. For the Lord said: *I ascend to My Father and your Father*.

Chapter 14. Always keep the fear of God in your heart, and remember that God is with you in every place, wherever you walk or sit.

Chapter 15. With His fear as a bridle, turn your mind and examine yourself constantly, lest you, walking without restraint, learn vain things.

Chapter 16. Bow your head to every elder with humility of mind, for by being humble, you will be exalted.

Chapter 17. Greet your friends, who are your equals, with love, and give them an embrace and a kiss, as Elizabeth did to Mary.

Chapter 18. Receive those younger or lesser in stature with love and mercy, and sigh to God on their behalf, for they are just beginning to know God.

Chapter 19. Fear the king with all your strength, for his fear is not for the destruction of the soul, but rather it teaches you to fear God.

Chapter 20. Neglecting the authorities is neglecting God Himself, who has established earthly authority. If one does not fear the visible ruler, how can he fear the invisible God?

Chapter 21. A student should fear the rod of the teacher, but even more the teacher himself. Likewise, one who fears the king fears God, for it is God who punishes sinners through the king. For the king is God's servant, dealing out both mercy and punishment to men.

Chapter 22. Bow your head in humility to every wealthy man. A great tree can be passed under by bowing, and you can move forward.

Chapter 23. He who receives power from his king demands glory from his peers and expects reverence from those lesser than himself.

Chapter 24. Always seek simplicity, both in food and in clothing. Do not be ashamed of poverty, for most of this world lives in poverty.

Chapter 25. And do not say, "I am the son of a rich man, it is shameful for me." For no one is richer than Christ, your heavenly

Father, who gave birth to you in the holy baptismal font and lived in poverty, having nowhere to lay His head.

Chapter 26. Adorn yourself with truth, strive to always speak truthfully to everyone, and do not be ashamed to face others, nor be a listener to lies.

Chapter 27. Fear to speak lies before the king, for the Lord will destroy those who speak falsehoods. But answer him with submission, as if to God Himself.

Chapter 28. If at any time you happen to speak falsely, without knowing it, fear God, for He may be testing you: whether you watch over your soul. If it becomes known that you have spoken falsely, and you cannot correct it, you are endangering your soul.

Chapter 29. If you speak the truth and fall into the anger of anyone, do not grieve about it; rather, take comfort in the Lord's words: *Blessed are they which are persecuted for righteousness' sake, for theirs is the kingdom of heaven.*[1]

Chapter 30. Be gentle with every person, both with those older than you and those younger. For feigned gentleness is when one is ashamed before superiors but oppresses those who are lesser.

Chapter 31. Let your walk be gentle, your sitting be gentle, your gaze be gentle, and your words be gentle. Let all these be yours, for by them a true Christian is revealed.

Chapter 32. Gentleness is not offending anyone, neither in word, nor in deed, nor in command, but sweetening the heart of every person with your ways.

Chapter 33. Always pull your mind away from vain thoughts and lift it up to God, for by this you will walk the path of struggle

---

[1]Matthew 5:10

and free your soul from slackness.

Chapter 34. It is not surprising for human nature to fall toward earthly things, but it is surprising when, having fallen, one does not rise again. For who, having strayed from the path, does not seek to find it? If the day has been weakened by despair, let tomorrow be a day of effort.

Chapter 35. Do not desire earthly glory in any matter, for earthly glory fades for those who love it. It passes by man like a windy storm, taking away the fruit of his good deeds and soon laughing at his foolishness.

Chapter 36. Foolishness is when, in expectation of the eternal blessings, the gifts of the good God, one does not wait with patience and faith, but rejoices in the earthly things, accepting them as if one did not believe in the resurrection.

Chapter 37. If the glory of the whole world had come near to the heavenly glory, the sons of this world would not have crucified the Lord of glory. For what servant dares to dwell in a house where his master was not received?

Chapter 38. Accept the dishonor of love as a cup of bitterness. Even if it seems vast to you, it will drive away the sinful sickness. For sin enters with sweetness, but departs with bitterness.

Chapter 39. Desiring eternal joy, partake little of earthly things, always thinking of your departure. Be not troubled by human reproach, for the Lord, coming into the world, endured dishonor from His own servant.

Chapter 40. Whoever seeks to be honored in this world cannot bear dishonor, but he who holds the faith loves dishonor. Remember what the Lord said: *How can ye believe, which receive honor one of another, and seek not the honor that cometh from God* *only?*

Chapter 41. Love hunger and thirst for the sake of Christ, and the more hardship you inflict on the body, the more grace you bring to the soul. The reward will be in accordance with your deeds, for He will repay good things for a little, for which we suffer with joy.

Chapter 42. Desire to rejoice with the martyrs for the sake of Christ. Give your body over to fasting, your will to being trampled upon, your stomach to hunger, your heart to strength, and pour out your blood. If not outwardly, then dry it up inwardly with the absence of food, so that you may receive the promised blessings.

Chapter 43. Know that those who invite the king cleanse their halls, and if you desire to receive the heavenly King into your house, cleanse your body with fasting for the light of your soul: destroy it with thirst, adorn it with humility, and incense it with fragrant prayer.

Chapter 44. Do not delay writing down the prayers of the soul, for just as the body mourns when deprived of food, so too the soul, deprived of the nourishment of prayer, approaches slackness and spiritual death.

Chapter 45. A candle is light in a house, and prayer is light in the soul. The light of the candle is bright and does not mix with anything else. Likewise, prayer is radiant, unsullied by earthly thoughts.

Chapter 46. Guard your candle from the wind, and your prayer from laziness. Adorn it like a bride with vigilance, labor, and patience, so that the heavenly King may desire it.

Chapter 47. Give your will to God, who knows all things before man exists, and do not ask for your will to be done. The thoughts of every man are unprofitable, but say to God, *Thy will be done*, for He does all things for our benefit, which we in the flesh do not know.

Chapter 48. Arise like the publican: run like the prodigal: be contrite like Ahab: weep like the harlot: cry out like the Canaanite woman: stand like the widow: pray like Hezekiah: humble yourself like Manasseh. If you pray in this way, the good Lord will accept your prayer, as a mother does her child.

Chapter 49. Find a secret place, and sit quietly. Remember your sins and the loss of the Kingdom of Heaven, and be moved with compunction in heart and in appearance. Bowing your head, say with groaning, *Woe is me, for my pilgrimage is far gone. Who will give my head water, and my eyes a fountain of tears? Alas for me, for the day is near.*

Chapter 50. If you do not have tears, do not despair, but sigh often and deeply, from your whole heart. For tears are a gift from God, and little by little, through sighing and contrition, you will ask them from God. For it is written: *Seek, and ye shall find; ask, and it shall be given; knock, and it shall be opened unto you.*

Chapter 51. Having found tears, keep them with all your strength, from gluttony, drunkenness, and especially from judging any man. Pay attention to your own actions, but do not judge the man whom God created.

Chapter 52. Do not trust your own eyes, even if you see someone sinning, for even they are unreliable. The eyes first caused the fall in paradise, and from their temptation, our downfall came.

Chapter 53. Judging the sin of another is the work of the sinless. But who is without sin, except God alone? For only He, being infinite, has the right to judge those who are under measure.

Chapter 54. He who bears on his ribs a wound full of pus is not disgusted by the impurity of another. Always thinking of the multitude of his own sins, he does not wish to discuss the scandal of others.

Chapter 55. Judging a man who has stumbled is pride and self-exaltation. But God resists the proud. He who constantly expects to give an account of his own sins does not quickly lift his head to look at the faults of others.

Chapter 56. Do not be proud, lest the grave boast of holding your pride, and the poor man rest on your grave until noon, suffering no harm.

Chapter 57. The worm is humble and lowly, but you are glorious and proud. Yet if you are wise, humble your pride yourself, remembering that your strength and your power will become food for the worms.

Chapter 58. Remember those who were once famous for their bravery, wealth, strength, and glory—how they disappeared without a trace and were forgotten. But the poor and humble in this world, who strove for their souls, are glorified in heaven, praised on earth, and called upon for help.

Chapter 59. Seeing a dead man being carried, have mercy on him, as he shares your nature, and follow him to the grave. You will receive two benefits from his death: you will remember your own end and be humbled; and by having mercy on his body, burying it in the grave, you will be shown mercy yourself.

Chapter 60. Visit the sick, and bring them whatever they desire to eat, and serve them yourself, as you would a relative, knowing that you will suffer likewise.

Chapter 61. When another groans heavily from illness, let tears of compassion flow from you, and sigh to God over his affliction. If a doctor is available, offer payment for his healing.

Chapter 62. When someone is dying, close his eyes and mouth with your own hands, and pray to God with all your heart for his soul. Wash your hands after. If he is poor, make every effort to bury him with dignity, even if he lacks anything.

Chapter 63. The time of death is urgent for repentance and tears, for who would not be moved by seeing his own nature entering the grave, his name extinguished, and his glory and wealth descending into darkness?

Chapter 64. If you have influence with the king or those in authority, grieve for the oppressed who suffer at the hands of the powerful. Fight for the orphan until you sweat, that the Lord may count your sweat with the blood of martyrs.

Chapter 65. If you do not know the king personally, appeal to those who do, and plead for the poor. The Lord will account this to you as He would the first.

Chapter 66. Incline your ear to the beggar, and to the one who has been impoverished in this life. Fill their lacking poverty with your abundance.

Chapter 67. Look mercifully upon one who sits in nakedness, shivering in the cold. Compel yourself to cover your own nature with the clothing that lies with you, and the Lord will give back to you a hundredfold and grant you eternal life.

Chapter 68. Stretch out your hand to one wandering the streets and bring him into your abode. Share your bread with him. Share your cup of water or drink, whatever God has given you.

Chapter 69. Bring the stranger into your house and the

homeless under your roof. Give the soaked one dryness, the freezing one warmth. Wash the filth from his body, for he is poor and worthy of mercy.

Chapter 70. Visit those in prison, as the Lord has commanded. See their sufferings and hardships, and sigh for them, saying, *Alas for me; these suffer for a single transgression, but I sin against my Lord Christ at all times and remain at ease.*

Chapter 71. If you see one of them suffering due to slander, help him for the sake of Christ, and reveal the truth to those who slandered him. There is no closer salvation for those near the king or noblemen than to deliver the wronged.

Chapter 72. While you sit at a table filled with many dishes, remember the one who eats dry bread and cannot bring himself water because of sickness.

Chapter 73. As you feed your body, give a portion of your table to your soul, for it is more precious than the body. Let the poor preserve the portion for your soul, so that when you seek mercy and God's help, you will find it ready at the hour of your departure.

Chapter 74. While you are filled with sweet drinks, remember the poor man drinking lukewarm water, heated by the sun and covered with dust.

Chapter 75. Being rich and having an abundance of earthly goods, always remember the word of Abraham to the rich man: *You received your good things in your lifetime, as the poor man received evil things. Therefore, he is now comforted, and you are in torment.*

Chapter 76. While you lie on a soft and spacious bed, remember the one lying on the bare ground, under a single rag, unable to stretch his leg due to illness and cold.

Chapter 77. As you lie under a sturdy roof and hear the sound of heavy rain, think of the poor who now lie pierced by raindrops like arrows, and others who, unable to sleep, sit and are lifted up by the water.

Chapter 78. While you sit in a warm room in winter, unafraid to undress, sigh and think of the poor who crouch beside a small fire, trembling, suffering more from the smoke in their eyes than from the cold, warming only their hands while the rest of their body freezes.

Chapter 79. Strive for spiritual things and think of spiritual things, not earthly ones. Knowing that by the incorruptible garment of baptism, all—both poor and rich—are equal, be careful not to despise the poor man clothed in perishable garments, thinking only in earthly terms.

Chapter 80. When the Church of God calls you to prayer, leave behind whatever earthly task you are doing and go diligently to feed your soul, as Peter and John did when they went to the Lord's tomb.

Chapter 81. As you go to the holy temple, think about whether you have angered anyone in any way. Make every effort to dispel the cloud of anger so that the light of prayerful goodness may shine on your soul like the sun.

Chapter 82. A dark cloud covers the brightness of the sun, and the remembrance of anger destroys the beauty of prayer.

Chapter 83. When you enter the doors of the church, in your mind pass through the very gates of heaven, and stand throughout the entire mystery with awe and fear, observing with faith both with your bodily eyes and your soul's eyes. In this way, you will be transformed from earthly thoughts to heavenly ones.

Chapter 84. When you see the holy and sanctified gifts being offered to God on behalf of all, lift up your hands to heaven and say with gratitude and faith, *Glory to Thy compassionate providence, O Christ God, Savior of the world.*

Chapter 85. Always reflect on your frequent sins and on God's boundless and innumerable compassion toward mankind, for He waits for repentance until the very last breath.

Chapter 86. Therefore, go before His face with confession, come and make haste, fall down before the Lord, and weep before the One who made you. Call upon His mercy, invite His compassion that death does not catch you unprepared.

Chapter 87. Do not say, *I have sinned greatly, and I have committed many iniquities; I have no boldness to fall before God.* Do not despair, do not add any more sins from now on, and with the help of the All-Merciful, you will not be put to shame.

Chapter 88. Do not say falsely: *He that cometh to Me, I will not cast out.* And after all these things, He said: *Turn to Me, and I will heal you,* for *I do not desire the death of a sinner.* Therefore, take courage and believe that you are cleansed, and He will cleanse anyone who approaches Him.

Chapter 89. If you truly desire to receive repentance, show it by your deeds: if you repent of pride, show humility; if of drunkenness, show fasting; if of fornication, show chastity. *Turn away from evil and do good.*

Chapter 90. But do not delay while stuck in the mire of sin, lest you suddenly sink deep. You will cry out, and there will be none to hear, when the angel of the Lord stands before your eyes, and your enemies will cover you like clouds.

Chapter 91. Take care of your soul, for it is the only one you have, and there is but one lifetime. You do not know the end, and the abyss of the air is impassable and filled with your enemies. There is no one to help you except your good deeds, so seek them with all your strength.

Chapter 92. Enter onto the path of virtue, and go quickly, before evening overtakes you. Strive toward the gates of the heavenly city, neither turning to the right nor to the left, so that you do not wander into the abyss of torment.

Chapter 93. Bow your head with all reverence to the bishops, the shepherds of Christ's flock, the rational sheep, and you will receive God's blessing.

Chapter 94. Honor and love the presbyters, the priests of Christ, the stewards of His mysteries, with all respect. Listen to them as they teach you the commandments of Christ.

Chapter 95. Likewise, show appropriate honor to the deacons, subdeacons, and readers, as ministers of God. Take care not to offend any of them.

Chapter 96. If you respect those who stand before an earthly king with fear, without contradicting them with your words, how much more should you respect the servants of the heavenly King?

Chapter 97. Visit monasteries and the houses of the saints. Observe their way of life, order, and structure, and seeing their dwelling, you will judge your own life and correct it from then on.

Chapter 98. Do not be lazy in going to those who dwell in the mountains. Seek their blessing and prayers. If you have any physical needs, bring them to them, and you will receive spiritual benefit.

Chapter 99. Above all, never pass by a monk without bowing. If you bow only to those whom you know and respect, it is merely fellowship, not reverence for the image of God upon them.

Chapter 100. The conclusion of all that has been said:

Love the Lord with all your soul, and let His fear dwell in your heart. Be righteous and true, obedient and humble. Lift your mind to heaven, having compunction for both God and man. Be a comforter to the sorrowful, patient in suffering, and never a cause of offense. Be generous and merciful, feeding the poor, welcoming strangers. Grieve over sin and rejoice in God. Be hungry and thirsty, gentle and kind. Do not be a lover of glory, nor a lover of money. Be a friend to all, without hypocrisy or pride. Be a striver toward God. In speech be sweet, in prayer frequent, in understanding wise, and in judgment merciful to every person. Be a defender of the oppressed. And you will be a child of the Gospel, a son of the resurrection, an heir of life, in Christ Jesus our Lord, to whom be glory and dominion, honor and worship, with the Father and the Holy Ghost, now and ever, and unto the ages of ages. Amen.